# AGAINST A RISING TIDE

# AGAINST A
# RISING TIDE
## Racism, Europe and 1992

MEL READ and ALAN SIMPSON

SPOKESMAN
for
NOTTINGHAM RACIAL EQUALITY COUNCIL
and
EUROPEAN LABOUR FORUM

First published in Great Britain in 1991 by:
Spokesman
Bertrand Russell House
Gamble Street
Nottingham, England
Tel. 0602 708318

Copyright © Spokesman 1991

Acknowledgement:
Roger McGough's poem 'There are fascists'
is taken from *After the Merrymaking*
(Jonathan Cape, 1971)
We are grateful for its use.

ISBN 0-85124-525-0 Cloth
ISBN 0-85124-526-9 Paper

Designed & typeset by Bromar Print
Printed by the Russell Press Ltd, Nottingham
(Tel. 0602 784505)

# DEDICATION

Wyn Williams was a former Chairperson of the Racial Equality Council in Nottingham, and a life long pillar of anti-racist and civil liberties campaigns. More than that, he was an educator 'par excellence' — encouraging, cajoling, infuriating and inspiring more people than it is possible to count.

Wyn died while this book was still in draft. It is a meagre tribute to a person whose dreams were always big enough, bright enough, resilient enough, to embrace us all.

# FOREWORD

This study puts into perspective some of the momentous changes facing the European Community, principally resurgent nationalism and increasingly overt racism. It also indicates that this is a time of great opportunity, provided that there is no retreat into prejudice, division, and discrimination.

There is a real chance to lay the foundations of a broader European Community and to lay to rest the legacies of fear and hostility.

But there is also a clear need for the means to be set out in simple practical ways. Alan Simpson and Mel Read have produced an important contribution to this process and I commend their work to you.

*Glyn Ford*
Leader of EPLP
European Parliament's Rapporteur on Racism and Xenophobia

# ACKNOWLEDGMENTS

Nottingham and District Racial Equality Council has the task of working towards the elimination of racial discrimination, the promotion of equal opportunities, and the building of good relations between people of different races.

These responsibilities required us to look at the implications of 1992 for black people. It began from fears expressed by Afro Caribbean and Asian groups, but it could not have proceeded without the commitment of Mel Read and the work done by Alan Simpson, our Research Officer.

We must also thank both the Nottingham City Council and the Nottinghamshire County Council for their support; the Churches Committee for Migrants in Europe for their help over international press coverage; the photographers who have let us use their work; and Carolyn Shield for her critical scrutiny of the whole process.

I hope that you find this book a good source of information, and an inspiration for practical action against racism in Europe.

*Greta Sahoy*
**Chair, Nottingham & District Racial Equality Council**
**Feb. 1991**

# CONTENTS

# INTRODUCTION

Most of us do not live our lives on an international or European scale. We get by on a more personal level; trying to ensure that, for us, in the words of John Dos Pasos, life can at least be "notafraid, nothungry, notcold: not without love" (The Big Money, 1936). It's not that bigger issues are unimportant: more that they so often seem inaccessible — beyond our influence.

The principle objective behind this study is of **empowering** people to influence changes that are already taking place. To do so we first need to be informed about the nature of these changes, their competing pulls and interests, and the dangers as well as opportunities that they present. We need to understand what is happening internationally in order to inform our actions locally — to know how local networks need to fit together into a larger process of influencing the direction of change in Britain and Europe.

There is also an important starting presumption that we need to assert in relation to the insidious presence of racism in our society. It is simply this — that, **within the context of a 'Peoples Europe', no one stands to benefit from the persistence of racism.** A rising tide of racial attacks, the exploitation (and super-exploitation) of migrant workers, the marginalisation of black people within the European Community, all serve to perpetuate deep divisions between us all. They leave black people as the principle victims and scapegoats of a society which is itself in a serious economic and social mess. Breaking through ignorance and prejudice is the first imperative in getting out of this mess. Doing this on a European scale presents an even bigger challenge.

No one should be in any doubt that the changes currently taking place in Europe will have the most profound effect upon our lives. Some, like the completion of the Single European Market by the end of 1992, have been in the pipeline for some time. Others, like German unification and the upheavals in Eastern Europe, are more recent, mesmerising and confusing. All, however, will bring substantial economic, social and political changes in their wake, including substantial and early mass movements of people across Europe.

1

We welcome the sense in which Britain must be drawn into a wider, more positive recognition of the complex, multi-cultured, many-raced world that we live in. What we are concerned about is the negative impact that some of the steps already taken will have on community life in Britain. In particular, we are concerned about the impact that the changes will have on the whole position of black people in Britain and in Europe.

It is, perhaps, understandable that most of the discussion around '1992' has focussed around economic issues. The Treaty of Rome was essentially an economic agreement. The Single European Act, which has to be complied with by the end of 1992, gives legal force to measures which will free up the movement of capital, goods, services and people around Europe, and which remove barriers to competition. The social dimension of this sense of 'greater Europeanism' has always taken a second place — lacking binding legal obligations, and deferring to the judgement of individual national governments as to what their citizens should be entitled to. But the legislation now being agreed to, and the private agreements being made by European Ministers, are taking us along a disturbing path; one

▶ which divides people living in Europe into 'nationals' and 'non-nationals';

▶ which risks fanning up the worst prejudices about 'foreigners' and 'migrants';

▶ which colludes with some of the most bitter and dangerous inclinations towards narrow nationalisms resurfacing throughout Europe; and

▶ which threatens to create a Eurocentric racism in which black people are increasingly carricatured as (unwanted) immigrants and refugees.

It is the danger, as Sivanandan described it, of spawning a racism

> *"which cannot tell one black from another, a citizen from an immigrant, an immigrant from a refugee — and classes all Third World peoples as immigrants and refugees, and all immigrants and refugees as terrorists and drug dealers ....."*

(New Statesman and Society 4 Nov. 1988)

Fundamentally, this report seeks to look at what we can do to prevent such a scenario. Initially, we have attempted to outline some of the economic, social and political underpinnings of the 'new Europe' we are entering; to examine the unholy alliance of new and old racisms which have conspired to produce an alarming upsurge in racial attacks across Europe, and the dramatic resurgence of racist and neo-fascist political movements in Europe.

As an Appendix to this report we have included the Recommendations of the Ford Report on Racism and Xenophobia which have been presented to the European Parliament. The Ford Report set out its own evidence of how far racist attacks have become common place across Europe, and how the Far Right are linking up internationally to promote the spread of racial violence, intolerance and intimidation.

Turning back this rising tide of racism will certainly require support for the actions that the Ford Report calls for at a European level. It also demands action at a national and local level; action in a context with recognises that the source of this racism is as strongly rooted in economic exploitation and the lack of social or citizenship rights as in actual physical attacks.

This is the context in which we attempt to make sense of 1992 and the Single European Act — and to prepare the ground for a Europe capable of fundamentally challenging the legacies of racism and fascism.

# EUROPEAN DECISION MAKING — TOWARDS 1992

## A PEOPLES EUROPE OR JUST A COMMON MARKET

When the Treaty of Rome was signed in 1957, it brought into being the European Economic Community. Its purpose was to create a common market for European goods and services: an environment in which business and industry could function without the bureaucratic irregularities or blocks thrown up by separate national governments in Western Europe. Although there have always been social objectives that the EEC has subscribed to, and which have a legal base in the Treaty of Rome, most improvements in the quality of life have been presented as by-products of economic harmonisation, integration and free competition.

To create this new environment, the Treaty of Rome established an independent legal system which was responsible for developing its own body of Community law. Such laws automatically apply to all Member States and neither require or allow for sanction by separate national parliaments.

Roni Alfandary

The **Council of Ministers** is where the real decision making power in European policy making resides. The diagram below sets out an outline of the way in which the European political institutions work and fit together.

# How The European Community Works

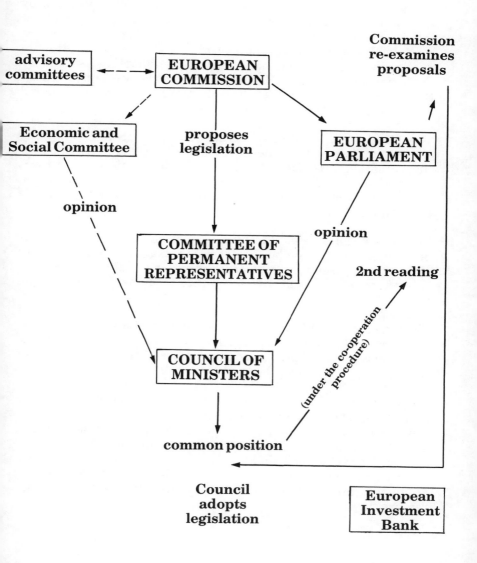

advisory committees ←--→ EUROPEAN COMMISSION

Commission re-examines proposals

Economic and Social Committee

proposes legislation

EUROPEAN PARLIAMENT

opinion

COMMITTEE OF PERMANENT REPRESENTATIVES

opinion

2nd reading

(under the co-operation procedure)

COUNCIL OF MINISTERS

common position

Council adopts legislation

European Investment Bank

The **European Commission** is the political 'think tank' of the Community, consisting of 17 Commissioners, including its President Jacques Delors. The Commissioners are appointed by the Member States but must swear on oath that they will act independently of purely national interests. The Commission is responsible for initiating and drafting legislation, monitoring its application, once adopted, and itself adopting secondary implementing measures. The Commissioners are supported by the Commission services, a relatively small civil service compared to national government departments.

The **European Parliament** is made up of 518 MEPs directly elected by the people of the 12 Member States. It has less power than a national parliament and cannot adopt legislation. It gives its opinion on legislative proposals, and in cases where the co-operation procedure applies, has two readings of the proposals and can exert more influence on them.

The **Economic and Social Committee** has 189 members nominated by the Member States and consists of representatives of three groups: employers, workers and various outside interests. It is a purely consultative committee, giving its opinion on proposals.

The **Committee of Permanent Representatives** of the Member States is made up of national civil servants and this is where the initial discussion of proposals takes place between the Member States.

The **Council of Ministers** is where the final decisions are taken and the legislation adopted. The Council consists of the relevant Ministers from national governments of the Member States, according to the subject matter under discussion. Thus, there is an Agriculture Council, an Industry Council, a Transport Council, etc. Some proposals are adopted by qualified majority voting, with voting weighted according to the size of the Member State; others require unanimity.

Within this structure the Council of Ministers, and to a lesser extent the European Commission, determines both the pace and direction of most of the changes taking place. This leaves the European Parliament in a much more subordinate role than you would normally associate with parliamentary assemblies.

Between them, the Council of Ministers and the European Commission have made a great deal of progress on the harmonisation of standards — of weights, measures, engineering and technical standards — and the European Commission now has its own bureaucracy for setting down the minutiae of trading regulations and standards. Little similar progress has been made, however, on developing the basis of the 'Social Europe' which was notionally part of the same starting agenda. There are, though, indications that political groups on the left in the European Parliament are putting increasing pressure for this process to accelerate e.g. via Directives on Protection for Atypical Workers, Protection for Pregnant Women at Work, and the Directive on Working Hours, which have now received formal approval.

For those who began with a vision of some sort of federal Europe — one which was able to make more equitable use of its resources and skills — there must be some degree of frustration and disappointment that the EEC's powers of compulsion and legislation have largely been used to strengthen the hand of European capital, without any strengthening of the rights of the 320 million people living within the EEC, to basic standards of housing, pay, health care, education or benefits. Directed 'progress' as such has been largely in the context of an integrated single internal market covering the 12 Member States, and in the growing debate about monetary union and a Single European currency. In that sense it is still more accurate to talk of these changes in terms of a common 'market' than a European community. The social dimension, is still a long way adrift from the main thrust of change in Europe.

The European Commission's response to issues of racism probably illustrates this better than anything else. In January 1990 Michael Elliott, one of the British Labour MEPs, gave notice of the following question at the coming meeting of the European Parliament -

> "Will the Commission, as a joint signatory of the 1986 Declaration against Racism and Xenophobia, indicate what specific policies it is proposing in the Action Programme of the Social Charter to help implement the objectives of the Declaration, and in particular as regards the need to eliminate all forms of racial discrimination?"

The Commission's response, whilst affirming its commitment **in principle,** and its belief that "there can be no 'Peoples' Europe' unless all citizens residing within the European Community live together in harmony", was a masterpiece of passing the buck. The way this was done was through what they refer to as the "principle of subsidiarity". In essence this means little more than that they have no particular political commitment to an issue. The EEC then leaves the responsibility for taking action to individual Member States. That way they remain honourably indifferent to the issues. Hence the reply that Mr. Elliott received -

*"In accordance with the principle of subsidiarity whereby the Community acts when the set objectives can be reached more effectively at its level than at that of the Member States, the Commission's proposals relate to only part of the issues raised in certain articles of the draft Charter. The Commission takes the view that the responsibility for the initiatives to be taken as regards the implementation of social rights lies with the Member States, their constituent parts, and the two sides of industry as well as, within the limits of its powers, with the European Community.*
***The Commission therefore has no proposals on discrimination on the basis of race, colour or religion."****

[European Parliament, Feb 1990
Reply to question from Mr. Elliott (H-102/90)]

Thus, the key decisions about social rights are still being taken by national governments. So much for the European Commission or the European Parliament leading from the front.

---

* Our emphasis

# EUROPEAN POLITICAL INSTITUTIONS

As a way of influencing the pace and direction of change, the structures of European decision making are remarkably obtuse. As the earlier diagram showed, there is a **European Parliament** to which all Member States elect their MEPs. This Parliament, with its 518 elected members has, however, no power to initiate legislation. It can undertake investigations, commission reports and have them debated in full sessions of the Parliament. It also has a number of **Standing Committees** which meet to discuss proposals and which can be extremely influential in pushing proposals for action and legislation. The main engine of change, however, undoubtedly lies outside the European Parliament. The **Council of Ministers** clearly holds the key levers of political decision making power. They can initiate legal change and they can block, amend or simply ignore, recommendations coming from the Parliament or the European Commission.

For those who are interested, there are already a great many very clear guides around the maze of European institutions*. The main point worth making at this stage, particularly for campaigning purposes, is the one frequently made by elected members of the European Parliament. At the moment there exists a very obvious "democratic deficit" within the European Parliament. The 'European' legislation which increasingly binds and compels Member States is not really shaped or determined by the European Parliament. So, whilst campaigns for change, must have an increasingly European or international focus, the key political players remain at a national government level. This is not to suggest that either the European Parliament, local MEPs, or the European Commission should be ignored in confronting the growth of racism in Europe. Rather it is to recognise the multiplicity of levels upon which this challenge must be built.

\*

**Some of the most helpful outlines include:**

▶ Working Together: the Institutions of the European Community, (Office for Official Publications of the European Countries, Luxembourg, 1988)

▶ Fact Sheets on the European Parliament and the activities of the European Community, (Office for Official Publications of the EEC)

▶ The EEC: a guide to the maze — Stanley Budd (Kogan Page Publishers)

▶ Equal Opportunity Implications of 1992: the Single European Market — the Association of Metropolitan Authorities, Second Report (June 1990)

# 1992 AND THE SINGLE EUROPEAN ACT

In 1985, Lord Cockfield the, then, European Commissioner responsible for the internal market produced some 200 proposals aimed at removing the technical, political, physical and fiscal barriers to trade. These proposals, in the form of a White Paper presented to the Heads of Government at their summit conference in Milan that year, were to ensure that goods, services, capital and people could move freely across the internal frontiers of Europe.

Eventually, 279 proposals became enshrined in the Single European Act which was signed in 1986, came into force in July 1987 and has to be enacted by the end of December 1992. There are 8 broad areas that the Act covers -

▶ **Simplifying and abolishing frontier controls on the movement of goods** — streamlining transit procedures and current customs arrangements within the EEC.

▶ **Technical harmonisation** — setting common standards for a wide range of European products which, if met, should make the products equally acceptable in all Member States.

▶ **Removing fiscal frontiers** — by harmonisation of VAT rates and rates of taxation on products and services.

▶ **Promoting industrial co-operation** — by harmonising the laws relating to patents, trademarks, etc., and by developing a common framework of European company law.

▶ **Freeing the movement of capital** — both in terms of access to loans and the international movement of money.

▶ **Extending the choice in business services** — including wider choice in banking and insurance services, and a liberalising of rules governing air transport.

▶ **Opening up 'public procurement' practices** — by removing national barriers in the awarding of supply contracts and public works contracts awarded within the Member States. This would also involve removing or reducing 'local preference' schemes run under national, regional or local initiatives, and promote community-wide tendering for major contracts; and

▶ **Freeing the movement of people** — by reducing internal frontier controls, removing restrictions on the right of citizens to live and work anywhere within the EEC, and offering mutual recognition of formal qualifications.

Many of these measures are broad and wide ranging. Others are highly specific and technical. All of them, however, will have the most profound effects upon the economic and social landscape of Europe.

# BRITAIN IN EUROPE
# — THE CONSEQUENCES
# OF FREE MARKET ECONOMICS

The elevation of free market forces, first as a moral imperative and then as a legal framework of Community rules, inevitably raised questions about the impact that this would have on national as well as regional economies. A series of EEC studies resulted in the publication of the **Cecchini Report** (1988), predicting a 7% growth in Community output and a 33% fall in European unemployment as a direct result of the single market. Since then, however, other studies have both challenged Cecchini's 'bottom-line' conclusions as being wildly optimistic and unrealistic, **and** have drawn attention to the much more adverse effects that even Cecchini acknowledged would be bound to happen in the short term. **Restructuring and rationalisations of production in all of the major industrial sectors in Europe will result in a rise in unemployment of over 500,000 people in the year following the completion of the Single Market.** The motor industry, textiles, the food industry and telecommunications equipment manufacturing were identified as areas likely to face 'painful restructuring'. The significance in the East Midlands of Plessey, the Toyota development in Derby and the traditional industries of textiles and footwear gives sharp focus to what this might mean.

What Cecchini and its critics also agreed upon was that the impact of restructuring will be uneven. It will hit small and medium size firms in marginal market positions particularly hard. The bigger firms will survive restructuring. The smaller ones may not. Large scale, multi-national capital will invariably emerge stronger, whilst the small firm may not emerge at all. Growth areas would prosper, whilst those in difficulty would face accelerated decline. Similarly at risk would be those firms within any given area which were working to a domestic market rather than to an export one, and firms which had a particular dependence on public sector contracts. In all, according to Labour's Brian Gould, there would be "a loss of 200,000 manufacturing jobs in Britain". (Guardian 16.9.89).

One study, the **Neuberger Report,** set the figures at slightly less than this but attempted to give a regional and sectoral dimension to the effects on UK employment and trade -

## Regional Impact of 1992

|  | Output percent | Total £m | Jobs(1,000s) Total |
|---|---|---|---|
| North | -0.8 | -129 | -8.4 |
| Yorks | -0.9 | -201 | -16.6 |
| E. Midland | -1.2 | -176 | -18.3 |
| E. Anglia | 0.3 | -97 | -7.3 |
| Gtr. London | -0.5 | -447 | -18.6 |
| Rest of S. East | -0.7 | -560 | -28.9 |
| S. West | -0.8 | -209 | -12.5 |
| W. Midland | 1.1 | -227 | -21.7 |
| N. West | -1.0 | -285 | -21.4 |
| Wales | -0.7 | -112 | -6.4 |
| Scotland | -0.8 | -237 | -14.1 |
|  |  |  | **-174.2** |

What is also suggested is that the sectors of industry most adversely affected in the UK would often see their output fall whilst the European output of their industries actually rose -

# EFFECT OF REMOVING TRADE BARRIERS IN THE UK AND THE EC

| Industry | Output % change UK | Output % change EC |
|---|---|---|
| Cement | -4.0 | 0.2 |
| Drugs | 0.5 | 0.4 |
| Office Machinery | -21.3 | 10.4 |
| Electric Motors | -0.1 | 0.4 |
| Artificial Silk | -6.7 | 4.2 |
| Machine tools | -0.2 | 1.7 |
| Carpets | -12.0 | 2.5 |
| Footwear | -15.0 | 3.2 |
| Electrical goods | -4.9 | 2.1 |
| Motors | -0.5 | 3.4 |

If we add these factors into the more specific picture of black employment in Britain, the economic scenario looks even less inviting. Whilst concentrations of black people in particular industries are important, far greater significance is their concentration in jobs which are unskilled or semi-skilled, temporary and, for women, part-time. Evidence in "Black and White Britain"* indicated also that black people are more likely to be unemployed — and to be unemployed for longer — than their white counterparts, comparing those with equivalent qualification and experience.

The last decade has seen deep changes to the structure of the British economy. The 'contract culture' and 'free market economics' have become a part of our every day life. They have brought great prosperity to some people, but have also required large numbers of people to be consigned to jobs characterised by combinations of low skill, low pay, no prospects, poor conditions, non-union and temporary, casual or unsocial in their hours of

---

* Black and White Britain — Colin Brown, the Policy Studies Institute 1984 — the third PSI survey

*Wanted — the work, but not the workers?*

work. The large pool of unemployed labour during most of the 1980s allowed the whole question of skill and industrial training to degenerate to the level of 'Magic Roundabout' government schemes; more about lowering wage expectations and 'parking' the unemployed out of the public gaze, than about raising the skill base of the UK economy. The painful consequences of this are now beginning to come through as we see a gap which has opened up between ourselves and our major competitors. The industrial levy system in Germany helps to ensure that 80% of its workforce have a formal skill qualification. This is almost a mirror image of Britain's position. **In Britain, 6 out of 10 young people abandon education entirely at the age of 16. In France, Germany and the USA only 1 in 10 do so.** Japan, Germany and France have twice the proportion of people undertaking higher levels of skill training and education as Britain has, while the USA has 3 times our level. Set alongside the serious decline in innovation and investment in manufacturing, this is one of the major structural weakness now built into the British economy. As the tables, below, illustrate, this deficiency in skill training stretches consistently across the major sectors of the British Economy.

## Engineers qualifying in western Europe

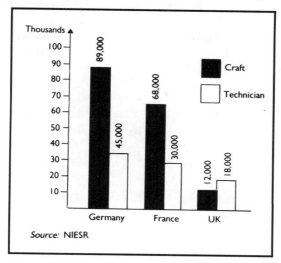

Source: NIESR

## Vocational qualifications in retail, 1986

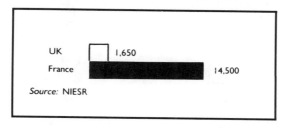

Source: NIESR

## Vocational qualifications in clothing, 1986

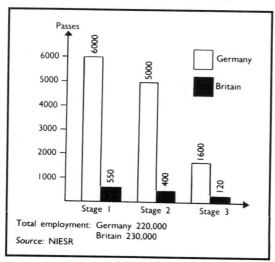

Total employment: Germany 220,000
Britain 230,000

Source: NIESR

The quantative and qualitative deficit in skill training in Britain is also reflected in the priority given to training in government investment policies. Compared to our major competitors, Britain is sadly adrift from the best practices in Europe and would need to spend an extra half billion pounds on skill training just to reach the average position of E.C. Member States. It leaves us singly ill-prepared for the full impact of the Single European Act.

## Government expenditure on labour market training for adults per employee, 1989

| | |
|---|---|
| Denmark | £164 |
| Sweden | £148 |
| Germany | £96 |
| Norway | £87 |
| Finland | £79 |
| Canada | £71 |
| Netherlands | £60 |
| **UK** | **£53** |
| Austria | £30 |
| US | £16 |
| Portugal | £14 |
| Japan | £8 |

For black people, the direct consequences of this scenario are particularly grim — over represented in the dole queues, persistently facing discrimination in both training and recruitment, and most vulnerable to redundancies in the mosaic of plant closures, lay-offs and company bankruptcies which newscasters drew and re-drew across our television screens during the decade. Black people have not been the sole victims of these changes, but they have often been singled out as the focus of blame for the plight that they and the country were in. They have also borne a disproportionate share of the negative economic and social consequences of these changes.

Whilst a similar pattern of events was also unfolding elsewhere within Europe, there were important differences. Economically powerless blacks in Britain appear to have civic and citizenship rights. In the rest of Europe black workers are mainly migrants with no necessary rights of settlement, housing, medical care or insurance. Increasingly they are also refugees, and asylum seekers with no legal status in the country.

As Sivanandan observed, in Europe -

> "... the new migrants are forced to accept wages and conditions which no indigenous workers, black or white, would accept. They have no pension rights, no social security, the employers do not have to insure them — they all illicit, illegal, replaceable."

(New Statesman and Society 4 Nov. 1989)

That is the most fundamental sense in which the growth of racism in Europe needs to be understood. The new imperative of silicon age economics is to have a highly stratified system of employment. Such a structure differentiates between 'core' workers — whose jobs carry with them status, security and civic rights — and 'peripheral' workers whose employment is uncertain and ill-paid, and whose rights are minimal, conditional and often inaccessible.

If this is the logic which underpins the Single European Act — if it is the underlying presumption of the European governments and multi-national companies who have championed its introduction — then the deteriorating position of black people in Europe becomes a 'functional' part of this process rather than an error or oversight.

The logic of a more integrated European economic system, one which would be able to take on the giants of America and Japan, would then be one not merely concerned with the economics of large scale production, and access to larger markets. It would be one which began from the implicit presumption that 'liberating the forces of growth' required an identifiable strata of society willing to undertake the lumpen tasks that respectable citizens would not entertain. This is the current position of the majority of migrant workers in Europe and, despite the formal citizenship rights that the majority of British blacks are currently entitled to, it is a very real warning about the pressures which are also coming to bear in Britain.

In the introduction to Gunter Wallraff's deeply disturbing book about the treatment of Turkish workers in Germany, Sivanandan wrote -

*"The racism that defines [the Turk] as inferior, fit only for dirty jobs and disposable, and locks him permanently into an under-class, is also that which hides from the public gaze the murkier doings of industry. And contracting out the shit work allows management itself to avert its face from its own seamy activities. That also saves it from the legal consequences of employing unregistered, uninsured workers and/or transgressing safety regulations — for these are the responsibility of the firm which hires out the labour.*

*But since the labour is alien, foreign, and therefore rightless, the law does not want to know. Nor does the government, which wants the work — cheap, unorganised, invisible — but not the workers ...*

*The whole system of exploitation is thus erected on the back of the foreign worker, but racism keeps it from the light of day. Is is the same racism, popular and institutional, that keeps the unions too from taking up the cause of foreign workers — and the contribution of the media and of politicians in making it popular, keeps them forever foreign."*

'Lowest of the Low', Gunter Wallraff (Methuen) p xiii, 1988

None of the advertising about Britain and 1992 addresses this aspect of the 'free market' equation. We hear a great deal about Europe being "open for business" in terms which always imply a rising prosperity for all. Free market economics have been dressed up as the embodiment of general well being. But beneath the glitter and the rouge there is a profoundly ugly and divisive dimension to European economic integration. A Europe fit for business offers no guarantees that it will also be a Europe fit for the people who live there (or would hope to do so).

Often it is easier to see the strains and contradictions in someone else's country rather than your own. If so, then Gunter Grass' critique of German unification, already running into the most serious of problems, stands as an object lesson for us all. Observing the revived and freshly developing hatred between Germans and Germans on the one hand, and Poles and Germans on the other, he commented

> *"I said that the Germans had lost their heads, taking no time to reflect and trusting only to the fetish of currency; involved in a unification process devoid of any joy; in which the larger partner dictates the pace and course of life in Germany.*
>
> *The smaller partner, whose inhabitants a moment ago were simply happy to be allowed at last to find themselves free from tutelage by the State, is now experiencing the dictates of profit orientated colonial masters, who were only prepared to invest when the bankrupt estate of the GDR had fallen to a giveaway price ....*
> *And now, once again, [the East Germans] are second class. Instead of a communist economy based on shortages, they are offered coarse exploitation under the label of 'Social Market Economics'. This unification looks ugly ....*
> *.... It is hurting those who are already injured and showing hardness towards the weak. Not only are they in the grip of unemployment but also growing to recognise that later on, when jobs are again available in return for low wages, the relationship of ownership will be clearly weighted in favour of West German capital. This certainty, already firmly rammed home, creates social envy which generally turns to hate."*

Gunter Grass 'The Business Blitzkrieg'
Weekend Guardian 20/21 October 1990

This is the ground upon which racism, anti-semitism and xenophobia flourish. It is by no means confined solely to Germany. A snails trail of bitter, intolerant and xenophobic movements is beginning to spread its way across the whole map of Europe — East and West. In all of such racist and anti-semitic movements, black people/jews/foreigners/migrants are offered as scapegoats for the deeper economic malaise that countries face -

*"As well as the mushrooming of the nationalist, racist and violently anti-semitic PAMYAT movement in the USSR ... the German Nazi 'Wiking Jugend' youth movement held a summer camp in the Soviet Union last year ...*

*"In East Germany last year there were 200 recorded incidents of racist incitement, and anti-semitic daubings have been found painted on walls in East Berlin ...*

*"... In Hungary and Poland anti-semitism has broken through to the surface with attacks on Jewish cemeteries. This anti-semitism has also been given official expression by Poland's powerful Roman Catholic Church, which defended the presence of the Carmelite nunnery at the Auschwitz death camp."*

('Nazism: a spectre haunting Europe for 1990'
Searchlight, Jan 1990,)

*Paris — members of an extreme right group near the Louvre.*

Anti-semitic outbursts in Poland are clearly symbolic of the deeper economic turmoil that the country is in. In an article describing the traumatic upheavals in the Polish economy in the "Independent", Hamish McRae commented -

> *"the central worry for Poland must surely be that the pain will last too long and the benefits come through too slowly; that people's patience will be exhausted. Although they have seen a savage cut in living standards, they have yet to lose their jobs. The most difficult change is yet to come ..."*

('Independent' 31.7.90)

In a country which had exterminated over 90% of its Jewish population before 1942 and now contains only a minimal number of Jews, the resurgence of anti-semitism in Poland is a remarkable example of what Shimon Samuels, European Director of the Simon Wiesenthal Centre, describes as "anti-semitism without Jews" (BBC Special Assignment Programme, Radio 4, 6 July 1990). It is a hallmark of societies seeking scapegoats for the deep economic hardships that people are being asked to accept.

Similar scapegoating and abuse is also reported to be taking place upon black workers and visitors in Eastern Europe, as the special relationships between the old regimes and emergent African nations begin to fall apart.

The anti-black and anti-semitic prejudices which have been unlocked in Eastern Europe can also be seen in every part of Western Europe; in a disturbing pattern of attacks, harassment and institutional and personal prejudice, as well as in the open emergence of Far Right, neo-fascist organisations. In the majority of cases of harassment or attack, black people have found that protection under the law is ineffective or non-existent. Many countries do not even recognise racial discrimination or define it as a crime. Those which do, often fail to credit it with any priority either in terms of enforcement or punishment.

Confronting the growth of racist and xenophobic movements does not figure anywhere in the language of the Single European Act; nor in the language of restructuring distinct national economies of East or Western Europe. It is, though, a sub-agenda to all of these changes. It is a sub-agenda which threatens to consign the 15 million or more black people in Europe to a sub-economic status which sanctions violence and intimidation against them, at the same time as nurturing their economic marginalisation and super-exploitation. If this is not the scenario we wish to construct for ourselves then **the establishment of fundamental social rights, the outlawing of racial discrimination and the development of effective anti-discrimination practices have to become a key part of the 'economic' imperatives of a broader, more tolerant, pluralistic Europe, rather than a social afterthought to it.**

# A 'PEOPLES EUROPE' — RACE AND THE SOCIAL DIMENSION OF EUROPEAN POLICIES

When he addressed the TUC Conference in September 1988, Jacques Delors, President of the European Commission, set out some of the key areas which, he felt, had to be developed as part of the social dimension which would run alongside the "irreversible" economic integration of Europe. He emphasised 5 main themes -

▶ the freedom of movement of people across national boundaries (with consequent rights to live and work anywhere within the Community),

▶ the establishment of a set of guaranteed rights — health, safety terms and conditions — for people in their workplace,

▶ the provision of high quality training for the unemployed,

▶ the development of a regional strategy within Europe to tackle marginalisation, under-development and economic decline, and

▶ guaranteed minimum rights providing every citizen with an assured subsistence income, and defined rights for all in relation to health care and public services.

The more detailed articulation of these aspirations came in the form of the "Charter of Fundamental Social Rights", unveiled by Ms Vasso Papandreou, the Social Affairs Commissioner, in May 1989. From the outset both the British government and representatives of British employers expressed equally fundamental objections to the notion of such fundamental social rights. A major collision of interests and basic philosophies was inevitable. What disappointed many people was that the Commission itself chose to narrow the ground upon which argument took place. Thus the 'Charter' which emerged concerned itself more with the particular rights of **workers** than the general rights of **people**.

*Roni Alfandary*

This is not to say that the Charter's contents were unimportant. They set out clear proposals addressing hours of work, freedom of association (in a trade union), fair and reasonable pay, free collective bargaining, worker participation in industry, health and safety, free movement of labour, sex equality and the protection of chidren and young people, minimum rates of social security, support for the elderly, training, and promoting employment of those with disabilities. The Charter, however, contained no mention of tackling racism, and ducked completely the racial divisions already being opened up between the categories of people living in Europe — **citizens, 'demizens'** (people with established residential and civic rights in one of the Member States but with 'Third Country' nationality) and **migrants** who, in essence, have no rights whatsoever.

Notwithstanding these massive shortcomings, the Charter was presented to the European Council of Ministers at their Madrid Summit meeting in June 1989. Britain stood alone in opposing its proposals and seeking to hold back any proposed 'rights' which might enter into the body of European law, in any way which compelled Member States to comply in strict terms.

The way Britain was able to do this was through "the principle of subsidiarity". In its Communication statement on 27th November 1989, on the development of an Action Programme relating to the Charter, the Commission trotted out the same line that it was soon to throw at Michael Elliott, MEP, —

*"The Commission takes the view that responsibility for the initiatives to be taken as regards the implementation of social rights lies with the Member States, their constituent parts and the two sides of industry\* as well as, within the limits of its powers, with the European Community.*

*"The Commission has, therefore, limited its proposals for directives or regulations to those areas where Community legislation seems necessary to achieve the social dimension of the internal market and more generally, to contribute to the economic and social cohesion of the Community. It mainly concerns proposals relating to social security for migrant workers, freedom of movement, working conditions, vocational training and improvements, particularly in*

*the working environment to protect the safety and health of workers.* **While the Commission is not making a proposal in respect of discrimination on the grounds of race colour or religion, it nevertheless stresses the need for such practices to be eradicated, particularly in the workplace and in access to employment, through appropriate action by Member States and the two sides of industry\*."**

(Commission of the European Communities,
Communication concerning the Action Programme
relating to the implementation of the Charter of
Basic Social Rights for Workers — 27.11.89 )

The general limitation of the Charter, then, is that it is largely left to the separate national governments to decide what they **wish** to implement. The principle of 'subsidiarity' defines the Commission and the European Parliament as not **competent** to specify the social rights which should be given to people within the European Community. 'Subsidiarity' demands that it will all be left to the separate governments, and that this freedom of action (or indifference) of Member States should be up-front, visible and spelt out in letters which are 6 foot high.

How different from the Single European Act, where economic sovereignty of national governments has been surrendered totally to a greater European 'market' framework, and strict laws and sanctions apply to those who would risk non-compliance. Free market competition is protected under law, public rights are not.

What is of equal concern is that the European Commission chose to define the responsibility for eradicating racism and racial discrimination as something beyond its general competence. This is particularly strange given that the Economic and Social Committee of the European Parliament had already set out its belief that racial equality had to be one of the "pillars of a social Europe". The Committee also stressed that **basic social rights had to be defined in terms which would have a meaningful effect on the lives of the most vulnerable groups within the Community — specifically "the disabled, migrants and ethnic minorities".** And yet, on precisely this pillar, the Social

---

(\* Our emphasis)

The general limitation of the Charter, then, is that it is largely left to the separate national governments to decide what they **wish** to implement. The principle of 'subsidiarity' defines the Commission and the European Parliament as not **competent** to specify the social rights which should be given to people within the European Community. 'Subsidiarity' demands that it will all be left to the separate governments, and that this freedom of action (or indifference) of Member States should be up-front, visible and spelt out in letters which are 6 foot high.

How different from the Single European Act, where economic sovereignty of national governments has been surrendered totally to a greater European 'market' framework, and strict laws and sanctions apply to those who would risk non-compliance. Free market competition is protected under law, public rights are not.

What is of equal concern is that the European Commission chose to define the responsibility for eradicating racism and racial discrimination as something beyond its general competence. This is particularly strange given that the Economic and Social Committee of the European Parliament had already set out its belief that racial equality had to be one of the "pillars of a social Europe". The Committee also stressed that **basic social rights had to be defined in terms which would have a meaningful effect on the lives of the most vulnerable groups within the Community — specifically "the disabled, migrants and ethnic minorities".** And yet, on precisely this pillar, the Social Charter flounders. It not only abrogates any responsibility for tackling racial discrimination, but it demonstrates a complete failure to understand the very nature of racism, and the shadow that it casts across the lives of black people throughout Europe.

The difficult challenge is to find a way of campaigning for the many good things in the Social Charter, without surrendering the need to build in specific commitments to strengthen the rights and security of minority ethnic communities throughout Europe -

*"It has been argued that the black population should embrace the Social Charter and support the campaign for it to be adopted as a declaration by the British government. At a national conference on "1992 and the Black Community" in Birmingham just before the elections, Euro MP Christine Crawley made it quite clear that the Single European Act should be seen for what it is: "the codification of a right wing philosophy of radical free marketism to deregulate Europe's economy in the interests of big business". At the same time she was emphatic that it would be a mistake for activists to therefore boycott any involvement in the processes leading up to 1992, as the Social Charter contained much of value. She felt that it was the most vulnerable workers — amongst them blacks and women — who had the most to gain from the protection of the Social Charter, "as they are the ones most in danger from the negative effects of the 1992 juggernaut". As black people are over-represented in the worst jobs, with the worst pay and conditions, then they are likely to benefit from anything which assists in the campaign to set minimum standards of pay and employment conditions, and counters the trend towards Britain's status as a low wage economy fit for social dumping."*

John Wrench — 'Europe 1992: The Single Market and Black Employment,' New Community, Jan. 1990

Whilst there is an argument about the need to change and strengthen European legislation, the growing evidence of racism — as prejudice, discrimination, exploitation or attack — has to be confronted as part of a programme of organised action at a local, regional and national level, as well as through more formal parliamentary channels. What the European Parliament could do is to give practical support for such work through its own budget and Action Programme.

Such a commitment would inevitably raise the lid on a whole series of issues about the treatment of black people in Europe, and of the treatment of migrant workers in particular; for it is in the context of economic exploitation that the expressions of racism and xenophobia are at their crudest and most stark.

## BELGIUM

### Opinion survey predicts upsurge of National Front:
The National Front is trying to project the image of a serious party in view of the legislative elections next year. Membership into the party is steadily increasing and an opinion survey (Iesop) indicates that 7% of the Brussels population is ready to vote for the Front (it received about 1% of at the last elections). New members are mostly those confronted with problems of insecurity supposedly caused by immigrants and are therefore attracted to this party's position on immigration. The party's leader claims that if they manage to "desatanize" their name, he is certain to the more than 10% of the votes."

Le Vif/L'Express, 27.7.90*

## FRANCE

### Life Sentences for 2 Racist Killers:
At the end of June, 2 young men found guilty of racist attacks against foreigners, causing one death, were condemned to life-long prison sentences. One openly advocated "the armed struggle" against the foreign "invaders" and regretted his "total failure" in planting a bomb in a bar frequented by North Africans which caused no victims. The other, who unfortunately 'succeeded', denied being racist. He tried with the help of false Jewish propaganda leaflets to make it appear as if Jews were responsible for his acts."

Liberation, 28.6.90*

*"Italy has become the latest battleground for the forces ranged on both sides of the racism argument. Florence has been the site of a number of violent incidents, with the local population venting their anger at Senegalese immigrants who sell cheap goods on the streets of the City ..... In 1989 one immigrant worker was killed and then burnt. He was a seasonal worker, picking tomatoes ..... Beneath his killing there was a very ugly story of exploitation and low pay and intimidation towards the numerous groups of black workers."*

BBC Radio 4 'Special Assignment' 6 July 1990

*"In one incident an Ethiopian woman, travelling on a bus in Rome, was thrown off her seat after another passenger said she was in a place reserved for whites."*

BBC Radio 4 'Special Assignment' 6 July 1990

*"There is a racial attack in the United Kingdom every 26 minutes. There have been 7000 racial attacks in London over the first 3 months of this year, according to figures from the Metropolitan Police."*

Glyn Ford MEP
Chair of the European Parliament's
Working Party on Racism and Xenophobia

# BLACK PEOPLE IN EUROPE

A long and protracted battle is being fought out between the governments of the Member States in the EC about the rights and status of black people in Europe. Many of the arguments are conducted in secret, and none begin from a desire to protect and enhance the rights of black people. They begin from the economic self interest of the separate governments.

They also begin from the difficult conundrum for governments that whilst the (cheap) labour of black people is needed, their physical presence (as citizens) is often undesired and unwelcome. The result is a complicated web of limited protection under the law and minimal to non-existent constitutional rights (as migrants or asylum seekers rather than citizens).

Roni Alfandary

29

# CITIZENS, FOREIGNERS AND REFUGEES

Britain's position in Europe is unique in two important respects. It is the only country to have offered citizenship rights to former colonial subjects. It is also the only country to have a comprehensive framework of anti-discrimination legislation on the statute books. Those with even the most remote knowledge of race relations in Britain know that both of these 'facts' are only worth mentioning in the most heavily qualified terms. The Race Relations Act (1976) is a most cumbersome and toothless piece of legislation. Its powers of intervention are limited; its powers of redress virtually non-existent. It encourages "good practice" — in employment, housing, service delivery, etc. — but has no real force to bring this into being. Worse still, it is used by the Far Right to persuade people that that's where all the jobs, houses, training, etc. have gone to.

In citizenship terms, the rights afforded to former Commonwealth subjects have been steadily and progressively reduced since 1948. There has been no new 'primary' immigration in Britain since 1971. The right to bring family and dependants to live together in Britain has become massively restricted and bureaucratically tortuous. As the CRE's investigation into the immigration services showed,* the **process** of dealing with claims for family unification and the acquisition of such (theoretical) citizenship rights, is itself riddled with racist practices and prejudice. There is a massive agenda about such 'rights' that Britain has yet to address.

Despite such heavy qualifications, a majority of the 3 million black people in Britain are now British citizens. However, there are still almost a million people in Britain who are classed as third country nationals. They are people who are citizens of another (non-EC) country but who are permanently settled here and who have **rights of residence** in Britain. This entitles them to work, housing, education, health care, pensions, etc. which are not legally restricted. The rest of Europe has no such arrangement and at the moment it appears that the rights of non-British citizens permanently resident in the UK will **not** be transferrable throughout the EC. The significant numbers of black people who fall into this category would, if they ventured into other parts of Europe, cease to be 'residents' and assume the status of 'migrants' or 'aliens'. The most obvious example of what this means is the position of Algerians in France.

---

*'Immigration Control Procedures' CRE, 1985.

Many Algerians will have lived and worked in France for over 25 years. None have any rights to take part or vote in local or national elections, After 1992, white British and French **citizens** will have an automatic right under Community law to move to any part of the EC, and to enjoy full social and employment rights there. This will not apply to the Indian or Jamaican national living in Nottingham any more than it does to the Algerian living in Marseilles. They will not have an entitlement to secure work in any other EC country. Moreover, if they did obtain employment it would be as migrant workers — stripped of social and economic rights. In Brussels they would find laws excluding them from living in parts of the city. From Bonn to Bologna to Bordeaux, they would be denied civic rights. Only Ireland, Denmark and the Netherlands currently give all residents — citizens and non-citizens — the right to vote in their local elections. Spain and Portugal do so in some circumstances but **only** where there is a reciprocal agreement. In Britain, the only non-nationals entitled to participate in local elections are Commonwealth and Irish citizens with established residence in the UK.

| | Number of resident non-community citizens | As Proportion of total population |
|---|---|---|
| Belgium | 315,200 | 3.2% |
| Denmark | 101,600 | 2.0% |
| France | 2,102,200 | 3.9% |
| Greece | 82,400 | 0.8% |
| Ireland | n.a. | n.a. |
| Italy | n.a. | n.a. |
| Luxembourg | 7,200 | 1.9% |
| Netherlands | 408,300 | 2.8% |
| Portugal | 65,700 | 0.6% |
| Spain | 140,400 | 0.4% |
| **UK** | **982,200** | **1.8%** |
| West Germany | 3,252,700 | 5.3% |
| **TOTAL** | **7,457,700** | **n.a.** |

NB the figures do not include members of ethnic minorities who are Community citizens.
Source: Demographic Statistics 1989, Eurostat.

As the table (above) shows, officially there are some 7½ million people in the European Community who fall into this category of being resident non-Community citizens. So far there is not the slightest indication that the European Commission or the Council of Ministers have any intention of coming up with a framework of legal rights which would place such legally settled, Third Country nationals within the EC on equal terms with other EC nationals.

*The daily trail of thousands of East Germans entering the West via Berlin. (1989)*

The existence of such a large number of (black) non EC citizens legally settled within the Community is a source of great confusion and conflict within the European policy making process. There may be considerable variation in the legal rights enjoyed by such third country nationals, but what remains consistent is that they bear the brunt of hostility, discrimination and economic exploitation in whichever country they are settled in. This makes the issue of racism in Europe far more complicated than the simple

'Fortress Europe' notion that some people have begun to talk about. Without doubt, there is a real risk that the development of common European polices on immigration, visas, and the treatment of refugees and asylum seekers will turn out to be no more than an amalgam of the worst prejudices and restrictive practices of existing Member States. There is a mountain of evidence which shows how far existing policies work to prevent or limit entry from black, Third World countries. The proof that such restrictions are about 'colour' rather than 'number' was made abundantly clear during the upheavals that have taken place in Eastern Europe. Before unification, the West German government absorbed a massive influx of people flowing in through its Eastern European borders. Most of these were from East Germany but many also came from Poland, Czechoslovakia and Romania. During 1989, 344,000 East Germans alone migrated across into West Germany. A million migrants were forecast for 1990 and at one stage the rate of entry of Eastern European migrants was in excess of 10,000 per day. Large numbers of East Germans were immediately given money, housing and offered work when they entered West Germany. They were also white, and considered by the West German government to be 'our people'.

Contrast this with the experience of black people in Britain. Thousands (not millions) of black Commonwealth families thought they had 'rights' to British citizenship — thought that they too were 'our people' — but have been stranded for years in queues outside Britain trying to find a way though the bureaucracy and obstacles devised to keep them out.

In that sense it is very easy to see the new Europe as a 'white club' — a fortress — which has one set of rules for migrants if they are white, and another set for those who are black. The rejection of Turkey's application to join the Community, (especially in the light of Mrs. Thatcher's encouragement of eastern European states to look to a future which they too were part of the EC), the conflict in the Gulf and in other parts of the Middle East, and an obvious upsurge in anti-Islamic feelings within Europe, all add to the momentum which seeks to describe Europe's future in terms which are increasingly white, continental and Christian. It is, in essence, the re-creation of Christendom.

The 'fortress Europe' notion, though, becomes less sufficient when you acknowledge that there are already millions of black people in Europe — as citizens and as legal residents — who will not be 'outside the wall' in any physical sense. Europe will still require their (cheap) labour. But the sense in which they remain outsiders needs to be analysed separately. The fortress image needs to be seen as an ideology or set of values that works internally as well as a set of barriers to the world outside.

# OUTSIDERS AND THE IMMIGRATION GAME

The EC is under enormous pressure to come up with a common policy in relation to immigration, refugees and asylum seekers. A number of factors contribute to this, most notably that part of the Single European Act (1985) which requires free movement of **people** as well as **goods** and **capital** — between EC countries. If internal frontiers and controls are to be relaxed then the pressure shifts to the Community's external frontiers and its immigration policies.

The changes taking place in Eastern Europe only add to the growing national (and EC) fears about the prospect of large scale population movements towards the EC. The Netherlands, Belgium and France have expressed fears of large scale migration from Poland if EC visa restrictions are lifted. Germany has agreed to set a quota on the number of Russian Jews it will accept and has warned that unless the Soviet Union is able to restrict the numbers of Soviet citizens leaving the country then Germany will have to review its visa policy relating to the USSR. The fear is that some 7 million Soviet citizens, fleeing from famine and social upheavals, might seek refuge in Germany or Austria.

Coming through the wall . . .

Outside the EC, countries such as Czechoslovakia and Hungary have joined Austria in expressing their own fears of mass population migrations towards the West, pointing to the growing numbers of Kurds, Indians, Turks and Romanians in their countries who are clearly waiting for the chance of clandestine migration into Germany.

On the other side of the EC, Spain has announced an amnesty for the 70,000 or more Moroccans who are living in the country, but has also announced tighter controls to restrict the entry of people from Morocco, Tunisia and Algeria. In Britain, 1990 saw a record number of asylum seekers attempting to enter the country. Despite a very tough line on visa restrictions, over 25,000 people had sought asylum here by the end of 1990. This included a significant growth in the number of unaccompanied minors who sought asylum in the UK. Some 2000 children (aged from 7 to 17) arrived from Eritrea requesting asylum. The Government claimed that such increased numbers were mainly 'economic migrants', simply looking for a better standard of living and are not therefore 'refugees'. Most of the Aid organisations working with asylum seekers pointed out, however, that they came overwhelmingly from the most strife torn countries rather than those which are simply the poorest.

The conflict in the Gulf, and the economic and environmental consequences it will have on Third World countries, will almost certainly add a further (huge) dimension to the complex picture of mass population movements that Europe (East and West) will have to address.

Within the EC, what has complicated matters even further (and has generated a massive amount of anger, debate and suspicion) is that **virtually all of the Groups working on common immigration policies are outside of the control of the European Parliament and European Commission. The separate national governments who have set up these working groups have reserved the right to keep their deliberations secret, claiming that they operate under international law rather than Community law.** On this basis, the European Commission has been excluded from the discussions on the argument that it is not 'legally competent' to have a say on such matters.

This has meant that much of the public discussion about what is going on has depended on information 'leaked' from these working groups. It says much for the Dutch system of parliamentary control (and much less for our own parliament) that so much of the information that has come to the public notice has done so through Dutch sources. It is worth simply setting out an outline of some of these key inter-governmental groups and the work they have been doing.

## The Trevi Group

This was set up in 1975 as an inter-governmental body which aimed originally at co-ordinating efforts to combat terrorism. It is attended by Ministers of the Interior and/or Justice of Member States within the European Community. Since 1975 the remit given to TREVI has expanded to include coverage of international crime and drug trafficking, and it has established 3 distinct sub-groups for dealing with these issues. In 1988 a further TREVI group was established to look at the problems of 1992 and the lifting of internal Community frontiers. Its aim was to standardise procedures and objectives for dealing with all the issues TREVI was addressing. This is where the most worrying and contentious issues arise about the linkage between refugees, asylum seekers and illegal immigrants on the one hand, and terrorists, drug smugglers and international criminals on the other. The scope for developing policies based on entrenched racial stereotypes is obvious.

Some of the measures being urged by TREVI include

▶ reinforced checks on persons at external frontiers

▶ an international data base and information exchange for Member States on people seeking entry to the EC, including lists of deported persons and personae non gratae.

▶ training of police officers for external border surveillance

▶ harmonisation of security measures and vetting criteria at ports of entry

▶ common legislation covering fines against carriers who transport passengers without adequate and/or valid travel documents

▶ the harmonisation of policies on immigration, visas and asylum.

# The Ad Hoc Group on Immigration

In 1986, at the behest of the British government (which then held the presidency of the European Community), this group was set up comprising of Ministers of the Interior. In this case, however, they also drew specifically on the assistance of senior officials from Ministries dealing with immigration.

The European Commission has a strange, and almost schizophrenic, involvement in this Group. It is there as a member in its own right but **not** as a 'Community institution' under Community law. (Since the Commission only exists as a Community institution this must be a very strange experience.) It does not therefore report what it is doing to the European Parliament.

There are 3 main areas that the Group has been working on -

1. A Draft Convention determining which State would be responsible for dealing with an asylum application presented in one of the Member States (and the applicability of its judgement throughout the Community).

2. A Draft Convention on all aspects of the checks on people at external frontiers, and

3. The preparation of uniform application forms for tourist and transit visas.

It is the last of these tasks — the issue of visa controls — which Member States have most seriously disagreed upon. They had to postpone the commitment to produce an agreed Convention on checks at external frontiers by the end of 1990. Many countries have serious differences relating to a common visa policy. Some governments believe that such a policy is of no real value without a common European foreign policy. This would require countries to agree on the desirability (or otherwise) of individuals, groups and nationalities. The possibility of such an agreement raises the most serious questions both about human rights in general and racism in particular. But the timetable for reaching agreement clearly left little time for public debate about the serious implications of any such Convention.

The latest information on the 'progress' on this Convention raises even more anxieties about the way in which Third Country nationals will be treated. Very much at the instigation of the British government, they have declared their

> *"intention to explicitly state that such nationals would not have the* **'right** *of entry',* even if they satisfy all the **conditions** of entry."*

Migrants Newssheet, Sept 1990

So, even if a person seeking to enter the EC had the correct entry visa, all the necessary documents setting out the purpose and conditions of the proposed visit, could prove that they had sufficient means of support themselves throughout the period of their visit, and could show they had the resources for their return journey (or travel to a non EC country), **they would still have no right of entry to the EC.** Other countries, notably the Netherlands, have argued that Third Country nationals with permanent residence rights in one EC country should have the right of free movement — even if this does not carry with it employment rights or is not guaranteed immediately.

Disagreements over a common visa policy are extensive and may still be far from any resolution. It seems certain that a fall back position will be for States to retain their own visa policies alongside a common European policy. Whether this will turn out to be even remotely practicable has yet to be seen. Either way it is unlikely to be to the benefit of black people seeking entry to an EC country, since the majority of countries from which visa restrictions are being lifted have been white and Eastern European, and those being added to the lists for visa requirements are mainly black and Third World.

# The Schengen Group

Schengen is the best known of the 'secret' inter-governmental groups set up by EC countries. It originally comprised 5 countries — Belgium, the Netherlands, Luxembourg, France and West Germany — who met in the Belgian town in June 1985 to sign an agreement on common border control and immigration policies. By the end of 1990, Italy had also become a signatory to the agreement and Spain and Portugal had been granted 'observer' status in the Group. The underlying principles of the 1985 agreement were

▶ firm immigration checks and controls at external borders, and

▶ the ending of checks at internal borders

Implicit in their agreement was that other, more systematic, ways of checking people's status within the 'free' area would also have to follow.

Again, although the signatories to this agreement are EC members, the Schengen Group works outside any framework of European Community Law. It does not, therefore, have to report its activities to the European Parliament.

The practical and political significance of Schengen is that it almost certainly has a pilot-function for policies which will eventually be aimed at the Community as a whole. Once 6 or more of the main EC states have agreed to a detailed framework of rules and procedures relating to relaxed control of internal frontiers, other EC countries will have little choice other than to fall into line or remain as outsiders. Any other Community-wide policy would have to begin from the enormous (unrealistic) task of unravelling Schengen before other alternatives would be considered.

A Supplementary Agreement being worked on by the Schengen Group set out 4 main areas of policy that were to be developed

▶ the reinforcing of external borders

▶ a common visa policy

▶ a common policy on refugees and asylum seekers

▶ a data-base system for collection and exchange of information on immigration related issues.

This has enormous implications for the rest of Europe and for those seeking to enter it for any reason. The only crumb of comfort is that the Schengen countries encountered serious difficulties in overcoming their own difficulties and reservations about the Supplementary Agreement and its signing was postponed from December 1989. West Germany had wanted East Germany included, — though unification has upstaged these arguments. The Netherlands wanted the harmonisation of asylum rules on entry and application to be extended to cover the **procedures** for dealing with asylum issues. Along with Belgium, it also had reservations about some of the human rights issues associated with the introduction of the personal information system. France didn't want an influx of Germany's unwanted immigrants or of the refugees from Eastern Europe.

Apart from Eastern Europe, all of these concerns are about the presence of black people in Europe.

The Schengen countries have now resolved many of their their differences and a modified Supplementary Agreement was signed in June 1990. German unification is now acknowledged. Commitments have been made to protect privacy rights in the information system. And any State has the right to re-examine an asylum application which has been turned down. They have also agreed to keep their policies on asylum seekers in line with the Convention drafted by the Ad Hoc Group on Immigration. What it does mean is that there is now a 'twin track' Europe where countries within the Schengen agreement will effectively lift their internal border restrictions, whilst other Member States — Denmark, Greece, the UK and Ireland — will maintain some degree of internal border checks.

## The Group of Co-ordinators
## (The Rhodes Group)

There are obviously only so many clandestine policy making groups that you can run before someone has to try and co-ordinate the polices they are producing. At its meeting in Rhodes in 1988, the European Council decided to establish such a co-ordinating forum. It is composed of senior government officials, and, because it was set up under European Community law, is able to be questioned by the European Parliament.

Its task is both to identify the obstacles to the complete removal of internal frontiers in the EC, and then propose a timetable of action for removing them. The work of the Group resulted in the production of the Palma Convention which set out such a list and timetable; dividing the measures into those considered 'essential' and those merely 'desirable'. This was signed at the Madrid Summit in June 1989 and, amongst other things, set out a **commitment to having a common EC visa policy in place by the end of 1992.**

Meeting this timetable is proving increasingly difficult. Britain is extremely hostile to any reference in the Convention which would imply free movement of Third Country nationals living in the EC. Denmark, however, wants the Convention open to non-EC States so that it can meet its obligations to other Nordic states. Many of the 12 Member States also wish to lodge their own reservations to the Convention which could reduce it to an absurdity.

The competing and conflicting interests of separate national governments make it difficult to see how such a common (or at least harmonised) immigration policy can be completed within the timetable that the European Council set for itself. As 'Agence Europe' pointed out

> "... it will be hard to catch up (before the 1992 deadline). All the more so because changes underway are bound to raise problems relating to immigration from these [Eastern European] countries, adding to those which more particularly concern immigration from the Mediterranean basin. It is clear that with the signing of the Single Act, an agreement should have been reached on a 'standstill', a high level scientific group should have been assigned with adopting principles acceptable to all from the point of view of ethics, traditions and objective interests, and then a common 'adaptable' policy should have been adopted.

> Exactly the opposite happened. Each one has tried to solve his own problems. Thus, in Italy, the parliament is on the verge of adopting a law that ... could allow the number of extra-Community immigrants to be doubled in a very short period time (including 850,000 clandestine immigrants) without the most elementary infrastructures to host them and offer them work. These immigrants will be 'parked' in Italy where they will then attempt to enter other Community countries."

Agence Europe, 26/27 Feb 1990

41

*The welcome on the mat*

*— East German refugees to the F.D.R.*

Consider, then, the different 'ethics' or 'principles' that Member States are working on. German unification ensures that former East Germans have full and unrestricted access to EC States. The German constitution also provides that "Aussiedlers" — those with German antecedents — have the right to return as full German citizens. Precise figures are hard to identify, but it is already being suggested that up to 3 million people currently living in the USSR,

Poland and Romania could exercise their right to live in Germany as full German citizens. The economic, social and political implications of this are substantial, particularly as these movements may take place over a short timescale due, partly, to food shortages and economic crises in Eastern Europe. There are, though, also consequences for Turkish people currently living in Germany. Their position is certain to be made more precarious as large numbers of 'migrant' Germans claim their citizenship rights.

Elsewhere, Denmark wants favoured terms for Nordic countries. Italy has rationalised a "problem" that it already had of illegal, black, migrant workers, but in a way which makes it obvious that immigrants are to be passed on to other EC States, rather than settle in Italy.

Virtually all Member States have major immigration fears, but there is a transparent apartheid in the way they are articulated. Migration from the Mediterranean basin (from Africa and the Middle East) is a problem to be blocked and restricted. Migration from Eastern Europe is a problem to be managed but incorporated. Mrs. Thatcher expressed the views of many of her European partners when she addressed the Czechoslovak parliament in September 1990,

> "We must create the sort of Community which you and others in Eastern and Western Europe truly want to join — a European Community which is fair, which is open, which preserves the diversity and nationhood of its members."

Guardian 19/9/1990

The 'welcome" on the mat is clearly white and (northern) Eurocentric rather than multi-racial and international.

---

* The Response to Racial Attacks and Harassment, Home Office, 1989

## FRANCE

**Court Equates Le Pen's Ideas with those of Fascists and Nazis:** Considering that there is a "troubling and essential similarity between the theories of Mr LE PEN (Chairman of the National Front) and those of fascists and nazis", a court in Toulon made the unprecedented move of establishing such a clear parallel between Nazism and the Front. It therefore ruled that the charge of defamation brought against an actor, Mr HANIN, who described the leaders of the National Front as "true Nazis" be dropped."

Liberation, 21, 22.6.90*

*"Stop animal experiments ..... use Turks instead"*

Graffiti on a wall in Duisburg-Wedau (Germany)
cited in 'Lowest of the Low'
-Gunter Wallraff (Methuen)

*"Refugees who have been housed in the London Borough of Bromley are facing racist abuse from residents. The housing department has provided homes for about 30 families, mainly from Somalia, Uganda and Iraq. Some of the refugees are victims of torture. One family was threatened by an openly racist man with two Rottweiler dogs. Other residents have made comments to the effect that housing is meant for local people."*

"Exile" — Newsletter of the British Refugee Council
July 1990

## UNITED KINGDOM

**Jewish Leaders complain to Home Office over upsurge of anti-semitism:** Jewish leaders, representing a community of about 350,000 in the UK, met with the Home Secretary MR. WADDINGTON, on 28.8.90 to express their grave concerns over the recent wave of anti-semitism. The meeting came days after a holocaust memorial in London was daubed with swastikas and the words "Jew scum". In addition, there have been 27 reported incidents against Jews and Jewish property in Greater London in the first 6 months of this year, compared with a statistically insignificant number in 1989. The incidents include a recent desecration of 25 graves in Willesden and the grafitti on the walls of a synagogue in Dollis Hill.

The Home Secretary is reported to have expressed his serious concern about the matters raised and emphasized the Government's vigorous commitment to tackling racial violence in all its forms.

Jewish leaders are, however, unhappy at the apparent unwillingness of the authorities to bring prosecutions for incitement of racial hatred on the publishers which is mainly aimed at the Jewish community."

The Daily Telegraph and The Independent, 29.8.90

# LEGAL RIGHTS AND RACIAL ATTACKS

Black people in Europe do have — at least in theory — some legal right of protection against racial discrimination. In most European countries the difficulty is that such rights are largely inaccessible, ignored or undermined. In one of the best summaries of legal rights of minorities in Europe Ansel Wong explained that -

> "In **Germany** the constitutional provision that prohibits discrimination has been interpreted as a declaration of intent. In **Denmark,** personal freedom, and in **Luxembourg** non-discrimination, are guaranteed only to nationals; in practice the government itself discriminates both legislatively and administratively.
>
> Few of the EC states have developed a comprehensive system of civil remedies.
>
> In the **Netherlands,** where there are laws that provide for compensation in the case of certain types of discrimination, these laws cannot form the basis of a private law suit: any legal action must be initiated by the public prosecutor. This is true of laws prohibiting discrimination in **Belgium** as well.
>
> The **Luxembourg** law against racism of 1980 does not permit associations combatting racism to bring civil suits. In **Denmark** there are no civil remedies available to the injured minority; while in **Greece,** civil remedies are available to citizens alone. And in **Ireland,** there is only a single statute prohibiting discrimination in dismissals from work that allows a private right of action."*

> Ansel Wong — '1992: opportunity or oppression?'
> in The Black Parliamentarian, 1989.

The absence of **civil** redress would be of less significance if a full panoply of **criminal** laws were being used to offer effective protection for minorities in Europe. This is simply not the case. Protection under the law is patchy and inconsistent.

---

* our emphasis                    45

*"**Ireland** has no special provision in its criminal code to combat racism at all. The **Luxembourg** law against racism of 1980 has yet to be applied. A **Greek** law punishes incitement to racial violence or hatred with two years imprisonment. **Belgium** law forbids public incitement to discrimination, hate, or violence against a person or group because of their race, colour, or national origin, and punishes those who publicly resolve to practise race discrimination. The **German** criminal code prohibits incitement to violence but contains no laws prohibiting acts of discrimination in public places or in the fields of employment or housing. The law in Germany, in fact, provides protection only to the Jewish population and does not address problems faced by other minority groups.*

*The Danish criminal code, in addition to punishing discrimination in the field of employment and in access to public facilities, fills in the gap left by laws such as the British one which punishes incitement because of the **effect** it may or does have on the public. In **Denmark,** it is a criminal offence to make threatening hateful or degrading statements about race, colour, nationality or ethnic origin with the intention of disseminating those ideas to a wider audience or in public — no matter what the effect on the public is or is likely to be. ..."*

*"... the **Dutch** penal code penalises racial insult, incitement to racial hatred, and discrimination and violence on the grounds of race, as well as the publication or dissemination of these ideas ... It is also a criminal offence in the Netherlands to discriminate against people on racial grounds, or to discriminate in the exercise of a profession or trade."*

*Ansel Wong, op cit.*

Two important factors are, though, missing from this catalogue of legislative provision. The first is that **there is an obvious and well understood gap between the law and its enforcement.** The failure of the police and the public prosecution services to protect black people is as well known in the rest of Europe as it is in Britain. In Britain at least, there is a growing recognition that this is the case and that, faced with the growing incidence of racial attacks, urgent action needs to be taken. This is the main thrust of the Home Office Report on Racial Attacks and Harassment*. It is also a key element in the discussions of Safer Cities Initiatives that are currently being promoted by the government, police and local authorities. The Ford Report on Racism and Xenophobia in Europe identifies a UK as now having one racial attack every 26 minutes. The problem simply exists on a scale which cannot any longer be ignored or tolerated.

The second important consideration is that, **elsewhere in Europe, it is virtually unheard of for anyone — black or white — to have a complaint against the police upheld.** In Britain, black people have a clear understanding of the racism which exists within the police force. They also recognise the extent to which the courts (and complaints procedures) trivialise or dismiss evidence of racial bias. But within Britain as a whole there is still a **presumption** of a public right to challenge prejudice, corruption, incompetence and misconduct within the police force. However inadequately this works, it does exist. In the greater part of Europe it would be regarded as pointless and absurd to pursue a complaint against the police through the courts. This does not, however, make Britain's record a good one. It merely makes common European action that much harder to develop.

The last 18 months have seen some of the most serious questioning in Britain about the interrelationship of racism and the police force. A string of court and press cases have highlighted the nature of the problems we face.

---

* The Response to Racial Attacks and Harassment, Home Office, 1989

In 1989, 70 year old Irvine Roberts received £5000 damages following an assault by the Metropolitan Police. It had taken him 7 years to get his complaint successfully dealt with. A 29 year old Nigerian woman in Hackney received £8000 damages having been raped by a Metropolitan Police Officer who told her that she would be deported if she didn't have sex with him. In October another officer from the Met was convicted after raping an 18 black girl in his police car. In December lay-preacher Rupert Taylor was awarded £100,000 (the largest damages award ever made against the police for a case of this kind) after drugs were planted on him in Notting Hill.

Such high profile court convictions are, though, quite rare. They are also merely the tip of the iceberg. Issues increasingly being raised by black and civil liberties organisations include questions about the fabrication of evidence to obtain convictions; the harassment of families who make complaints against the police; harassment of those involved in campaigns against unjust convictions or improper arrests; and harassment of black people in the ordinariness of their everyday lives. The sad thing is that it is only when celebrities or sportsmen, like former world boxing champion Maurice Hope, or world indoor 200 metres athlete John Regis, express their own frustrations of being fed up with being abused or set up by the police, that the general public takes any notice.

One way of beginning to tackle this would be to change the system of dealing with complaints against the police. During 1989 there were 21,825 complaints made against the police in England and Wales (excluding London, which accounts for a further 12,500 complaints). Of these, more than 1 in 4 are complaints of assault.

Only 3% of the complaints against the police are upheld. Complainants are never told what disciplinary action or punishment follows, and most complainants also add that the police are actively unhelpful and discouraging when people attempt to register a complaint against them.

The credibility gap is even wider in relation to complaints about racism in the police force. In London, during the 3 years from 1985 only 3 such complaints were upheld out of a total of 394. In an interview with New Statesman and Society, Sir Peter Imbert, Commissioner of the Metropolitan Police added his own concern about the low percentage of such complaints which were upheld. He did not accept that 99% of complainants were lying about racist police behaviour, saying *"we are failing because officers are committing those offences, and we are not doing anything about it. We are not getting them."*

Sir Peter Imbert, quoted in 'Checking the Bill'
New Statesman and Society, 12 Jan.1990

There are two obvious aspects of the existing procedures which need to be changed. The first is the establishment of an **independent complaints procedure.** Sir Peter Imbert himself acknowledged that there is such a serious lack of public confidence in the existing complaints procedures, and that changes have to be made

*"If I could be persuaded that there were those who could investigate as effectively as police offices, I see no reason why there could not be independent investigators."*

Sir Peter Imbert, New Statesman and Society (op cit)

The second change concerns action taken on the complaints themselves. At present, any complaint is only upheld it if is able to be proved 'beyond reasonable doubt'. The police have been extremely good at closing ranks on this issue. It makes the burden of proof so stacked against the complainant that any doubt at all is sufficient to reject a complaint. Many people have argued for a long time that all non-criminal complaints should be determined on 'the balance of probabilities'. This would give the complainant a fairer chance of having their complaint recognised and redressed.

In cases where the complaint is about criminal behaviour then there is no real alternative to more effective pressing of charges. In such circumstances the refusal of police officers to give evidence should be regarded as both a dismissal offence **and** grounds for prosecution for conspiracy to pervert the course of justice.

The urgency of making such changes is not simply in terms of tackling racist behaviour within the police force. It is to recognise that the way in which the police deal with issues of racism also effects the climate of racism in society as a whole. If racism is an accepted part of the 'canteen culture' inside the police force, then those who are the victims of racial attack and harassment outside are likely to see the sentiments of their attackers reflected in the indifference or hostility of the police response itself.

It has fallen to groups like CARF (the Campaign Against Racism and Fascism) to set out the links between such locally based harassment and a wider European agenda. They argue that -

*"The police are adopting a far more authoritarian — indeed colonial — attitude towards the policing of inner city areas whose communities are seen as a threat to a system divided between the haves and the have nots. This public order policing — itself a product of government policy — is likely to get worse with the advent of 1992 and the European Single Market. In fact (although there is no political or public debate on this), 1992 is being used by the police to press for the formation of a national police force to fit into a European policing federation (rather like the American FBI system). Policing is becoming more centralised, more secretive and, as European states themselves pass racist laws and are faced with intractable regional and 'immigrant' problems, governments are increasingly turning to the police to solve political problems. Collaboration between European police forces can be witnessed by the fact that police from Germany, Denmark and Sweden attended this year's Notting Hill Carnival. And senior police officers are deeply involved in European initiatives such as Trevi (on terrorism, drugs and illegal immigration). New legislation on policing is also in the pipeline.*

*The effects of this are already being felt on the ground with the targeting of black, migrant and refugee communities. A Government White Paper, published in January, revealed big increases in resources for the policing of immigration. The trigger for this crackdown, particularly on the Sanctuary Movement, was given in December 1988 with the police dawn raid on the Church of the Ascension in Manchester and the subsequent deportation of Viraj Mendis. Large-scale raids against Turkish workers have been carried out in Hackney and Wembley since then. And activists involved in the Sanctuary Movement also report break-ins, surveillance and evidence of telephone tapping.*

*The targeting of black housing estates has also been carried out throughout the year on the pretext of looking for hard drugs (an operation on the Heath Town Estate, Wolverhampton and the Broadwater Farm Estate, Tottenham being the most notable examples). No such raid has secured a substantial seizure of hard drugs and seizures of small amounts of cannabis surely cannot justify the huge public expense with which these raids are carried out. In fact, all these raids serve to do is to further embitter communities who do want action on drugs but do not want to see the harassment of whole communities."*

Searchlight, Jan.1990

It is not appropriate here to go into a detailed examination of the ways in which racism operates within the structure and working practices of policing in Britain. What is important is that we understand that -

(a)    **the persistence of bias and bigotry within the police force is a major obstacle to effective action against racial harassment in Britain as a whole**

(b)    **political changes in Europe are also influencing the philosophy and organisation of policing in the UK**

(c)    **the lack of effective redress against racially biassed police actions (or inaction) both encourages racial harassment and further undermines the position of its victims, and**

(d)    **the development of any common visa policy which relaxes or removes internal frontiers in Europe, will inevitably lead to an extension of police powers (and resources) aimed at the internal monitoring, primarily, of black communities.**

There is a growing fear that, across Europe, black communities will face the compound problems of economic exploitation and marginalisation, growing vulnerability to racial attack, and an increasing sense in which they are seen (and policed) not as citizens deserving protection, but as archipelagos of illegal immigrants — the locus of problems rather than the focus of prejudice.

This is a message that the Far Right in Europe have already picked up on all too clearly. Their strategies, however, differ according to the circumstances in different countries.

## UNITED KINGDOM

**Another Jewish Cemetery damaged:** During the weekend of 28/29.7.90, the Jewish cemetery in Charlestown, Manchester was desecrated with swastikas and anti-semitic slogans on graves. A number of tombstones were smashed and broken. There have been at least 5 similar attacks on Jewish Cemeteries, mainly in London and the South East, in the past 3 months."

The Independent, 30.7.90*

**IN THE CAMDEN AREA OF LONDON the number of reported racial attacks on Asians has risen by nearly 130% -**

*"We have now several attacks every week upon Asian people, many of whom are simply going about their days life — returning home from school, going to do the shopping — and they are beaten up, assaulted, occasionally so seriously that they suffer fractured skulls. And when they're at home they're attacked with having their windows broken ..."*

*"The racists dislike having Asian people living on their estates. They dislike the resources diverted — quite properly diverted to provide them with accommodation, to provide them with schools, even to provide them with a Bengali club. And because of this resentment it gives them the excuse to try and attack them to try and drive them out of the estates."*

Chief Superintendent Peter Stevens, Camden Police
Radio 4, 'Special Assignment'
July 1990

## FRANCE

**Extreme Right Police Inspector Expelled from Force:** The Secretary General of an extreme right police union (FPIP) that is close to the National Front, Inspector LACANU, has been formally expelled from the police force. Mr. LECANU, who is also a member of the extreme right PNFE and responsible for the setting up of the neo-Nazi "Special Section" (SS) along with 4 other police officers, was imprisoned last October in connection with his alleged involvement of the bombing of an immigrant hostel and of the office of a magazine in 1988."

Le Monde, 13.6.90*

## BERLIN JUDGES CONSIDER VOTING RIGHTS FOR FOREIGNERS AS UNCONSTITUTIONAL

The participation of foreigners in local elections is, according to majority of the judges of the federal administrative court in Berlin, unconstitutional as the word 'people' in the constitution should be understood as 'the people of the State' i.e. the German people.

Local autonomy is an activity which can only be legitimised by German people living in German municipalities.

from Die Welt 12.2.90*

# The Far Right in Europe

Within the rest of Europe Far Right organisations have found themselves differently placed than their counterparts in Britain. Neo-fascist and neo-nazi groups in Britain have temporarily withdrawn from any formal political arena. The official demise of the National Front in January 1990 marked its terminal decline in popularity amongst Far Right activists. Long gone were its heady days of fielding candidates in political elections. From its position of putting up 303 candidates in the 1979 General Election, and getting 190,747 votes, it disintegrated to a handful of divided and disgruntled followers. In the last dozen years strategy has changed and new groups have emerged to ferment racism and harassment in different ways.

*National Front at the Cenotaph 1988.*

Instead of the pursuit of electoral support, the Far Right have taken to the streets in more cynical, seditious and intimidating pursuit of black people. Sometimes they do so by incitement, others by direct action themselves. The British National Party, the National Front Flag Group, and the really hard line groups of Column 88, the League of St. George and the Clarendon Club, have taken their activities down to a grass roots level, where physical intimidation and the fanning up of localised hostility towards black groups is now far more important to them. John Tyndall, former Chairman of the NF, had no doubts about why 1979 was the key to the NF's terminal decline. The Front itself was bitterly divided. Its electoral campaigns were marred by brick throwing rallies and demonstrations. And most important of all, the defection of many 'constitutional' extremists to a Conservative Party which increasingly looked much closer to their own views.

> *"The Tories under Thatcher appeared to adopt a lot of our policies. She talked about Britain being swamped, and a lot of people inferred she would do something about it."*
>
> John Tyndall, Independent, 17 March 1990
> ('When Tories fade, fascists take heart')

Tyndall argues that disillusionment with the Conservatives in the 1990s will lead to a new 'era of opportunity' for the Far Right in electoral terms and cites the developments in the rest of Europe in support. But the largest and most active groups on the British Far Right have become internationalist in a very different sense. Their links have been with the network of European terrorist groups with a long record of brutal and cynical attacks to their names. The anti-fascist magazine 'Searchlight' has a remarkable record of documenting and exposing these links and the atrocities perpetrated by such groups. They have also set out how electoral respectability under different European voting systems have given the Far Right a public platform they have not enjoyed in Britain. It has also given them access to public funds to promote their pernicious campaigns across national frontiers.

*NF march — London 198*

The most obvious example of this is in the events which have followed in the wake of M. Le Penn's election to the European Parliament. Le Penn has consistantly used both the resources of the European Parliament and the immunity from prosecution which goes with his status as an MEP (Member of the European Parliament) to ferment racist and xenophobic divisions wherever he has had a platform. His FN (Front National) party has provided support for the Frente Nacional in Spain and the Front National in Belgium. Though notionally a 'respectable' political party, the French FN has a history littered with racial violence. Le Penn himself has been convicted in the French courts for inciting racial hatred, and members of his party have been convicted of arson, of blowing up an immigrant's house, and of blowing up a café in Annecy. In April 1986 an FN member was charged with the murder of a French Socialist. There is a long record of firearms and assault charges against FN members. In 1987, following a speaking tour undertaken by Le Penn, there was a wave of attacks against North Africans and other immigrants. Following his rally in Nice, where Le Penn was apparently given a huge welcome, a Tunisian was murdered.

*Le Pen bodyguards during Paris March 1988.*

During the summer of 1990, the strong anti-semitic part of extreme Right Wing activities in France culminated in growing wave of attacks upon Jewish people and synagogues, and the desecration of the cemetery at Carpentras where a body was dug up and impaled on railings.

The rewards for the Far Right and for M. Le Penn and his Front National Party in particular, have been a rising success rate in both national and European elections. Over 2 million French votes ensured that they hung onto their 10 seats in the European Parliament. Success in French Parliamentary by-elections has been even more resounding -

> *"... the FN, headed by Jean-Marie Le Penn, grabbed a staggering 61% in Dreux in Normandy and 47% in Marseille in the south.*
>
> *The candidate in Dreux, Madame Marie-France Stirbois, was elected in a second round run off against a member of the conservative Gaullists ... Madame Stirbois became the first fascist to be re-elected to the French Parliament. Her campaign was organised to follow a viciously anti-immigrant and racist line in a city that has 11,000 North African and Turkish immigrants."*

Searchlight Jan.1990

*Children of the far right — Paris 1988.*

An almost immediate consequence of the FN's success was the tightening of anti-immigrant polices of the French Socialist government. The French Prime Minister promptly reported that France had deported or refused entry to over 76,000 foreigners that year and that plans to give settled immigrants in France the right to vote in local elections had been scrapped.

No doubt drawing on wider events in the Middle East and a growing wave of anti-Islamic feeling, many of the attacks and hostilities in France have been targeted at Muslims from former French colonies in North Africa. It is a disturbing pattern which can also be seen emerging in other European countries. Florence in Italy has been the focus of a growing wave of violence against North African immigrants in the city, most of these migrants earn their living as street sellers or as super-exploited workers in a rapidly growing underclass in the Italian economy. Last year, in southern Italy, a Senegalese man involved in seasonal work as a tomato picker was murdered and his body burned. In Rome, an Ethiopian woman was thrown off a bus by someone proclaiming that she was sitting on a seat reserved for whites.

In electoral terms in Italy, this undercurrent of racial hostility finds expression in the votes — almost 2 million of them — which went to the neo-fascist MSI Party. This was despite the MSI being in organisational disarray following the death of its leader Giorgio Almirante.

In other parts of Europe the fascist movement still remains small but growing. In Belgium the 'Vlaams Blok' won their first seat in the European Parliament, and in the Netherlands a long time neo-nazi was elected to their national parliament. It is, though, in Germany where the most disturbing changes are taking place.

In 1989 the neo-nazi Republikaner Partei (REP) — led by former Waffen SS General Herr Schonhuber — sent shock waves through the German media, when it won 11 seats in the West Berlin city parliament. Two months later its equally hard-line rivals, the National Democrats (NPD) won seven seats on the Frankfurt city parliament. Since then Republikaner have also won seats in local elections in Cologne, Dortmund, Stuttgart and Mannheim. In the European elections Republikaner took 6 seats as the largest section of a combined fascist vote in Germany of 2,655,000.

This development in Germany has to be seen in the context of German unification. The lining up of anti-black and anti-semitic groups across former German frontiers is already well underway. Nationalist hysteria in East Germany clearly gave the green light to a whole range of Far Right groups which have been responsible for the desecration of Jewish cemeteries as well as attacks on Vietnamese and Mozambiquan workers.

Gunter Grass, one of Germany's most distinguished and outspoken novelists, set out his fears about the rising tide of racism and xenophobia in the new Germany; a Germany which he described as driven into unification but without unity.

> *"Already the West German radical Right, which only a short while ago was split by disagreement, has united with the East Germans: they are proclaiming a revival. And since hatred only languishes as self-hatred in individual cases, it looks for targets outside the ranks of its own people: anti-Polish hatred is already a daily phenomenon west of the Oder ...*
>
> *... everywhere in the region near to the border there is a concentration of xenophobia — usually directed more at Vietnamese and Africans — aimed directly at Polish guest workers and Poles in general ...*
>
> *I fear that the economic differences between East and West, augmented as they are by deep-rooted nationalism, will result in violence — although the scope for practical hatred between rich and poor Germans, and even poorer Poles, is relatively slight compared with the complex multifariousness of the opportunities for hatred which presently exist between the industrial nations and the peoples of the Third World."*

Gunter Grass, 'The Business Blitzkrieg'<br>Weekend Guardian, 20/21 Oct 1990

Nowhere is this battleground going to be more obvious than in the turbulent economic upheavals in a Germany which is physically united but deeply divided in terms of wealth, class and race.

*East London 25.Nov.1990*

Also anticipating some of the enormous economic difficulties which will follow from German unification is Herr Schonhuber, who confidently now predicts that his Republikaner party which will be the main beneficiary of the collapse of the East German state, and the almost certain demand of 'German jobs for German workers'. Equally certain is that those who will be amongst its principal losers and victims will be the non-white and non-European residents in Germany.

Not only does the Far Right in Europe operate in an increasingly internationalist and integrated way. It also has a twin pronged strategy — **participation (and success) in electoral politics is constructed on the back of locally based agitation around economic, housing, education and amenity issues and a rising tide of harassment and intimidation against black, migrant workers and their families.**

This is also the writing on the wall for Britain. It is what people here need to weigh up as we move steadily into the New Europe of 1992 and beyond. As British Euro MP, Glyn Ford, warned -

> "... in Britain we should not be complacent about the lack of electoral success of fascist groups in this country; well over 7 million people across the EC voted for openly fascist or racist candidates in the June (1989) elections. And this success has, if anything, increased in the last 6 months."

> Glyn Ford — 'The Growth of Racism and Fascism in Europe'
> European Labour Forum, Summer 1990.

In his report on 'Racism and Xenophobia' to the European Parliament in September 1990, Mr. Ford and his Committee of Inquiry go much further than warning about the dangers of complacency. They argue for a comprehensive European programme to counteract the spread of racism, anti-semitism and xenophobia. What is more important about their findings and recommendations (summarised in Appendix 1) is that European action has to be based around local supportive action which challenges the social isolation of migrant communities, challenges their economic marginalisation and exploitation, and guarantees them the full civic rights and protection they should be entitled to. Protective legislation at a European or national level has to be fought for, but the challenge to racism has also to be **worked** for at a local level — within the bread and butter issues which shape peoples lives and perceptions.

*Tours August 1990. Anti-National Front demonstration. (Francois Guillot)*

In doing so we will also have to confront issues unaddressed by the Ford Committee, namely

▶ the implications for a growing European dependence upon an underclass of black migrant labour, and

▶ the alarming prospect of widespread racial conflict being sparked off if Europe is caught in the downturn of an economic recession.

Moreover, we will need to do so in Britain with a clear understanding of the "new era of opportunity" that John Tyndall and elements of the British Right hope will come in the wake of increasing economic difficulties. In their relaunch of the NF under the banner of "The Third Way" the New Right are looking for a sanitized image for old style prejudices. As one of the Third Way candidates (a former member of the NF directorate) explained to the press -

> "We want to protect small businesses, the self employed, worker-owners. We believe in decentralisation, village life, that there's no such thing as Britain. It is a family of nations, Welsh, Scots, Yorkshire, Ulstermen ... On race we support ethnic separatism and we've developed links with Muslim separatists. We'd consider putting to the public whether compulsory repatriation was necessary or correct."

Independent 17 March 1990

The 'greening' of the New Right opportunistically combines work with animal rights groups (on anti-halal meat campaigns) with support for separate Muslim schools (merely to reinforce the notion of Muslims as outsiders in Britain). Behind the community – based and ecological facade, however, little has changed. As in France, Germany, Belgium, Italy, Spain and the Netherlands, the electoral prospects of such 'sanitized' Far Right parties still draws heavily on the spread of violence and intimidation, division and hostility. It's principal targets are still black people.

This is what we have to draw up strategies to counteract.

There are fascists

"there are
fascists
pretending
to be
humanitarians

like
cannibals
on a health kick
eating only
vegetarians

Roger McGough

## THE NETHERLANDS

**Increased discrimination against Moroccans and Turks:**
Moroccans and Turks are increasingly discriminated against in the city of The Hague. During the first 6 months of this year, there were 388 complaints filed at the centre for registration of discrimination, compared with 475 during the whole of last year.

The complaints concern conflicts in neighbourhoods and at the workplace, and it was mostly Muslims who suffered from bad treatment. The discriminations include the sudden end to long-standing employment contracts. A possible explanation might be the fact that racist parties are represented in the municipal council which encourages some people to be openly against foreigners.

Whether ethnic minorities should be concentrated in certain neighbourhoods is the subject of a lively debate. Some take the view that concentration gives better opportunities for integration whereas others believe the contrary and plead for ethnic minorities to mix with the native population."

De Volkskrant/NRC, 98.8.90*

## ITALY

**Four Simultaneous Bomb Attacks:** In December, bomb explosions when off at the same time at the entrance of 4 houses in different places near Naples. The Houses were all occupied by non-EC foreigners, but there were fortunately no injuries.

Il Manifesto, 11.12.90

## ITALY

**Building Chosen to House North-Africans Destroyed:**
The city administration of Turin decided to use an abandoned school as emergency housing for North Africans. As soon as the decision became known, the building was destroyed on the night of 23.12.90.

La Stampa Sera, 24.12.90

## FRANCE

**Paratroopers Organise a 'Beating of Arabs':** In the small town of Carcassone where a regiment of paratroopers is stationed alongside an important community of Harkis (French nationals of Algerian origin who sided with the French during the War of Independence), a group of about 50 of them went into an area inhabited by Harkis and immigrants and beat every Arab in sight with chains, bars and other arms. The preceding Sunday, one member of their regiment almost had his throat cut in a fight with a young Algerian.

The inhabitants who are dependent on the presence of this regiment were hardly disturbed by the incident which many consider to be no more than youthful pranks. As for the local administration who has condemned and expressed regret over the incident, it refuses to label it as racist.

Liberation, 21.11.90

# LOCAL ACTION IN A EUROPEAN CONTEXT

## a campaign framework

*"The truth is that the European population is as unintelligent and politically illiterate about the subject of race as the English population has been. In 1992, there will indeed be movement of white and black people across the frontiers but that will not, by itself, dispel the racist ideologies that thrive everywhere."*

Ranjit Sondhi — The Spread of European Racism in 1992
in '1992 and the Black Community' [Kaamyabi]

What we want to do in this section of the report is to look at some of the practical steps we might take to help dispel such racist ideologies. Using Nottingham as an example, we want to look at ways in which local anti-racist action might be developed in a European context, and can then be dovetailed into campaigns at a national or international level.

*Festival against racism in Paris 1988.*

64

# A LOCAL FRAMEWORK

Even thinking about action against racism on a European scale is difficult. The extent of the problems in Europe and the remoteness of the levers of power to influence events can seem daunting. Yet it is precisely at a local level that the most effective work can and must be done to combat racism. The activities of Far Right and extremist organisations may be increasingly co-ordinated at a European level, but their actions are still very much focussed around localities. In response, we need to develop a social, economic and political climate in which racist agitation cannot survive or thrive.

Much of this can be built upon ground work that has already been done in Britain. The anti-deportation campaigns organised within different cities, by different trade union and voluntary bodies, and across different regions, are excellent examples of such work. So too is the work being done in different cities to combat racial harassment, and work on discrimination in employment and training. It is also evident in national campaigns against racist immigration laws. What we must begin to do, however, is to re-focus such work; to put it into a more co-ordinated framework of action and understanding. In part this means co-ordinating action on three key areas upon which racism operates -

1. the threat to personal security

2. economic exploitation and marginalisation, and

3. the denial of civic or citizenship rights.

Many of the best examples of work being done in Britain to combat racism, still focus on these as separate issues. We end up with important initiatives which suffer from being disconnected from the broader alliances which urgently need to be built for a more concerted attack on racism.

The other part of a re-shaped framework for anti-racist action is that we need to look at ways it can tie in to similar work being done elsewhere in Europe, so as to develop an international perspective on the challenge to racism. This should include initiatives which link work going on in different cities around Europe.

It could also embrace joint initiatives between cities, regions, trade unions, churches or local communities. It could focus on ways of exerting pressures on those who are making national or European decisions about future policies and practices relating to race relations. It could look for resources to co-ordinate action programmes against racism.

There will be no single blueprint for such action. Many areas around Britain will already be involved in significant work to combat aspects of racial discrimination and intimidation. This existing work will clearly shape the decisions that different localities make about their most appropriate starting point for putting work into a European context. One thing is certain though:- **there has to be a local lead and a local structure given to co-ordinating a programme of work against racism.** An example of what has been happening in Nottingham, and how it might develop, may help put this in a more practical context.

In July 1990 the Nottingham Racial Equality Council jointly sponsored a Conference in the City on Race Issues and 1992. It was co-sponsored by the City and County Councils. What made the Conference of particular value was that the City's 'European Unit' had contacted one of its twinned cities — Karlsruhe in Germany — asking if they wished to be involved. They were unable to do so but telexed over a proposal for a "Common Declaration Against Racism", in which they stated -

> *"The signs of racism and hostile behaviour are increasing in the Federal Republic of Germany. Groups and parties who are interested in racism use existing prejudices, fears and tendencies for their political targets ....*
>
> *The Municipal Council is very much against all movements to disturb the long and good corporate life between foreign fellow citizens and fellow citizens ...*
>
> *The democratic parties in the City of Karlsruhe will prevent every start, now and in the future, to cleave asunder the German and foreign inhabitants of our town ..."*

see Karlsruhe Declaration, (Appendix 2)
July 1990

This proposal opened up a whole new dimension to the notion of 'twinning' links. It also begged questions of how people in Nottingham, and other local authorities, could respond. In many ways the Karlsruhe Declaration parallels the 1985 European Declaration Against Racism and Xenophobia. It is a statement of principles, with a general commitment to take action against racism, but with no specific 'action programme' attached to it.

The second Report from the European Parliament on Racism and Xenophobia (The Ford Report) has now presented a much more specific agenda and timetable of proposals to be included in the European Commission's own 'Action Programme' and budget. There is a need to explore the possibility of echoing such action at a local level. The possibility of using the network of twinning links also offers a way of developing and sharing such action in an international context. If Nottingham is to respond to the Karlsruhe Declaration then the local authorities and local communities must now draw up their own list of specific commitments which they would wish to offer in any twinned and common action programme against racism.

# THE BASIS OF A COMMON AGENDA

a)  As with most British cities, Nottingham has a long record of supporting race relations work. Both the City and County Councils also have a record of support for black community projects. But real work on tackling racism and discrimination is a comparatively flawed, and often contentious, matter.

The experience of developing such policies is also something which could be positively shared between British cities and their twinned partners elsewhere in Europe.

Both local authorities serving Nottingham have Equal Opportunities Policies. Both have begun to monitor their own recruitment and promotion procedures. One has a formal 'recruitment appeals procedure' for dealing with racial bias in advertising, shortlisting and interviewing. The other has set up its own positive action training programme (an alternative to Employment Training) which offers targeted training for specific vacancy areas in local authority services. In both cases there are consultative arrangements with representatives of groups active within the black communities. Such consultations also look at detailed aspects of service delivery — in education, social services, leisure, housing, and cultural or artistic activities.

These 'consultations' have not fundamentally altered the balance of power and inequality in the local economy, but they have been an important channel for doing some of the work that is actually listed in the Ford Report on Racism and Xenophobia. It is also an area where, in both the public sector and the private sector, substantial work has been done by trade unions; getting their own members to press for effective equal opportunity policies in their place of work.

In pursuing and sharing such initiatives, it is important to remember that, in other parts of Europe there appears to be a much more limited legal recognition of racism as 'discrimination' — in jobs, training, education and services. Nor is there a common practice of consultation with ethnic minority communities, in ways which shape and monitor policies which affect them. This is something positive that many British authorities could productively build upon in their links with sister cities inside and outside the European Community.

b) One of the most consistent points of criticism raised within local black communities has been the lack of support they have been able to receive for dealing with immigration and deportation issues. During one of the campaigns against racist immigration laws — in which trade union branches and the local TUC combined with black and anti-racist groups — the Nottinghamshire County Council set up **a fund for supporting legal challenges to discrimination in immigration and nationality cases.** In European terms, such public support — for contesting visa restrictions, the denial of immigration rights, and limitations upon freedom of movement — will become increasingly important. It is as essential to promote and develop such support mechanisms in other European cities and regions as it is in this country.

c) Racial harassment and intimidation is not new but is always traumatic. It is also now recognised to be increasing at an alarming rate. The machinery for dealing with racial harassment needs to be dramatically improved to deal with this.

In the early 1980's Nottingham's Housing Department responded to longstanding criticisms from local communities about racial bias in housing allocations. By 1985 they had extended this work to incorporate racial harassment. A very clear policy statement was produced, the offence of 'racial harassment' was spelt out in tenancy agreements, and a structure of responsibility for dealing with complaints was set up for housing management staff. It remains the clearest of policy statements in any of the City or County service departments.

However, there is still a serious gap between the policy statement and effective practical action by the Authority. In response to the growing incidence of racial violence a much more co-ordinated approach is now being developed. This includes -

▶ the setting up of 'pilot projects' by the County Council in two multi-racial areas, in which local managers of different services are brought together to develop intervention strategies which will give immediate support for the victims of racial attack **and** take effective action against the perpetrators.

▶ both local authorities — along with local community groups, the police and the Nottingham Safer Cities Project — are working on detailed ways of combatting racial attacks, and

▶ the Nottinghamshire Police Force have accepted the definition of the Association of Chief Police Officers in which they now recognise that racial harassment includes -

> *"any incident in which it appears to the reporting or investigating officers that the complaint involves an element of racial motivation; or any incident which includes an allegation of racial motivation made by any person".*

The local police have also been issued with a new Force Order setting out their responsibilities for dealing with racial harassment or attack. As with the local authorities, the acid test of this will be the extent to which it becomes part of everyday policing practice, rather than merely a statement of intent.

These initiatives are, though, important things to share with other areas that local authorities are twinned with. But, in themselves, they are an insufficient response to the problems we have to confront.

▶ Whether this is part of a 'twinning' process or not, work has to be undertaken on a number of areas which will have wide reaching implications. These are best expressed in the form of specific recommendations for a local action strategy to combat racism -

**ACTION NEEDED**

1. There has to be a co-ordinated (and resourced) political lead given by local authorities to combatting the growth of racism.

2. The Intervention strategies should have a common monitoring format and an independent evaluation system.

3. Black community and anti racist groups must be involved in drawing up, monitoring and supporting such strategies.

4. Resources must be found, not only to give effective support to the victims of racial harassment and attack, but also to mobilise local community support for action to combat the spread of racism.

This point is particularly important in that neighbours and the local community are often a more immediate and practical source of support and action against racism than are public agencies.

In Nottingham's case there are serious shortcomings in current local authorities arrangements for tackling issues of racism, namely -

5. **The City Council's involvement is desperately short of a clear political lead.** Their European Unit staff and those from specialist departments, have given considerable support to the development of efforts to combat racism. But this is both unco-ordinated and limited — without a consistent lead from senior elected members of the authority.

The County's position is almost the opposite. Elected members have taken the lead but there is an unclear officer structure to follow this through. We would therefore urge that

6. **A European Desk or European Unit be set up within the County Council and that a Senior Officer be designated to take specific responsibility for the development of its action programme to combat racism,** and

70

*Equal rights and anti-racism — France 1990.*

7 **Community involvement is immediately built into the planning of action strategies in the pilot areas identified by the Council.** This needs to be done at the start, not tagged on as an afterthought once the County has worked out what it intends to do.

8 **Community Conferences or Seminars should be held by the local authorities (initially on a quarterly basis) to outline and review progress being made. Such meetings should be chaired by the local MEP and, if possible, resourced by the European Commission.**

9 **Resources should also be made available to support local community involvement in at least 3 areas of work**

a) **national campaigns to promote equal rights in Europe,**

b) **involvement in the development of the European Migrants Forum, and**

c) **the promotion of anti-racist programmes within existing twinning links.**

10 **Groups of MEPs should also be asked to sponsor Regional Conferences which attempt to share and build upon common experiences in the development of effective strategies to combat racism.**

It is impossible to draw up an effective programme of action aimed at countering the rising tide of racism without addressing the role of the police. Everyone should be entitled to full protection under the law. The trouble is that a large (and growing) proportion of black people have come to believe that the police are often

▶ indifferent to the complaints of those who are victims of racial attacks

▶ inclined to side with the attacker(s) rather than the victim(s) and

▶ directly responsible for some of the racial harassment which takes place.

The police clearly have an enormous amount still to do in building up public confidence in their ability to work in an effective and non-racist way. The historic result of the industrial tribunal case brought by PC Surinder Singh against the Nottinghamshire Police Force gives an indication of just how much work there is to do. At the end of the longest and most expensive industrial tribunal in British history, the police were found to have racially discriminated against PC Singh.

More than that, a succession of police witnesses provided ample evidence of the extent to which racist language and abuse permeated the canteen culture of the force. For most black people this will come as no surprise. It was merely surprising to see it come out into the open!

This is the way in which the police see and treat their fellow (black) police officers. The tribunal did not even begin to examine police treatment of black members of the public. It is not for this Report to suggest how local police forces should begin to put their own house in order. What we do urge is that,

▶11 Local authorities must ensure that their monitoring of racial incidents covers the adequacy of the police response to complaints, and the extent to which the victims of racist attacks end up being the ones who are prosecuted by the police.

Throughout this Report we have been conscious of the need to address racism on several fronts at the same time. You cannot separate issues of personal safety from those of economic exploitation or of the denial of civic and social rights. Only by addressing the issue at the level of root causes, is it possible to make serious inroads into the areas where racism thrives. In tackling such root causes it becomes possible to build up links, alliances and support for other groups of people who are similarly exploited, oppressed or harassed.

It is also possible to identify some of the broader problems (and possibilities that local action programmes to combat racism might seek to address -

## Italian youths beat Tunisian in third attack on immigrants

George Armstrong and Reuter in Florence

A GANG of youths beat a teenage Tunisian with iron bars in Florence's most famous square yesterday, the third attack on north African immigrants in the city in six days.

In the first of the earlier attacks, masked soccer hooligans, armed with baseball bats, beat up a Tunisian during all-night carnival festivities on Shrove Tuesday. An attempt to stab him was thwarted by the arrival of other carnival revellers.

Residents in the Santa Croce district also reported attacks on other immigrants by youths on Friday night.

Police have identified the baseball attacker from his record of brawls at the football stadium. Since he is still a few weeks away from his 18th birthday he has not been detained and says he will do it again.

In another racial episode on Sunday night in Piazza della Signoria, Florence, arrests were made.

On Ash Wednesday, Parliament approved, after a long debate in the press, a law that allows Africans, and others now in Italy clandestinely, to make their status legal by April 30.

Entry visas will become much easier to obtain.

They will have free medical care and lodgings are promised.

Elsewhere in Florence graffiti have appeared saying: "Jobs for the Italians — bashings for the blacks."

Guardian 6.3.90

## Poverty and Unemployment

At least as many black people are trapped in poverty in work as poverty out of work. The facade world of current government training schemes mainly fuels the supply of cheap labour into highly marginal service work. In most British cities this is the position in which disproportionate numbers of black people are trapped. There are many who argue strongly that this is by design rather than accident -

*"What the new economy needs, and creates, is a small core of highly skilled workers who are able and versatile to handle a range of tasks, while the rest of the labour force is discarded. The long grim lines of workers disappearing into foundries and factories before the break of dawn and reappearing at night are a thing of the past. It is out of these 'rejects' that a new servant class arises — hairdressing salons. This is the rise of the new entrepreneur, fighting in a fiercely competitive world for custom, for personal liberation from a lifetime of unemployment."*

Ranjit Sondhi (op cit. p.23)

74

It may simply be stating the obvious, but in today's highly service-orientated economy such 'one man bands' are just as likely to be women.

Ways of tackling such economic marginalisation are not easy to identify at a local level. However, it is possible to see ways of making some progress in terms of **training**. One possibility is

12 **Local authorities, trade unions and community organisations should now press for more appropriate skill training programmes which move into line with the higher standards (and rewards) set by Britain's major competitors.**

The targeting of such training initiatives then becomes an element which needs to be openly monitored in any local action programme. At the very least, local authorities can establish 'good practice' models of training schemes offered to black people which also address the authority's own recruitment needs. Thus

13 **Local authorities should develop their own 'positive action' training programmes targeted directly at minority communities, and structured around the skill areas where shortages and recruitment difficulties are already evident.**

14 **Local authorities, the trade union movement and local communities should also play an important role in identifying key areas of employment which marginalise and exploit black workers. This could go on to support pressures to improve pay and conditions associated with such employment.** Given the record in Europe of treating 'foreign' guest-workers as illicit, disposable and dirt cheap, there is a real need for intiatives to expose and prevent such inimical practices.

15 **Local authorities should include community representatives in discussions with local employers, negotiating targeted pre-entry schemes for jobs which offer more substantial pay and career opportunities.**

# Civic Rights

If local authorities (and local MP's and MEP's) are to effectively offer support to all of those who live in their area then

**16 Local authorities should offer direct and indirect support for efforts to secure equal civic and citizenship rights throughout Europe.**

This may range from affiliation to national campaign programmes to the setting up of local immigration appeal funds. It has, however, to be taken up as a matter of urgency if 1992 is not to present black people with only second class tickets for the European train that everyone is apparently trying to clamber on board.

All of these areas can be undertaken entirely at a local level. They should certainly enlist the support of local MP's and MEP's as well as the trade union movement. But they must, pivotally, develop a broad base of public support from which to work. The most obvious opportunities for fitting this into an international context is in respect of **twinning links.**

**17 Local authorities should seek to establish 'common declarations against Racism and Xenophobia' with the areas they are twinned with.**

**18 Such 'declarations' should be accompanied by 'action programmes' which set out aspects of work which would be tackled by the respective cities/regions.**

**19 Each 'action programme' should have its own clearly defined timetable for implementation.**

**20 The development of 'action programmes' must be built on the involvement of local communities as well as public agencies.**

**21 Resources must be found and mobilised to support people-to-people involvement in the development of twinned programmes to combat racism.** This is of enormous importance since church, professional, community, education and trade union organisations often have twinning contacts, and programmes of their own which can go well beyond the scope of formal exchanges between public bodies. Such work will often need resources, though, to allow it to develop its full potential.

## DENMARK

**Asylum seekers evacuated after violent attack:** Asylum seekers accommodated in the seaside resort of Gilleleje have been moved to a more secure place following an attack at the end of July but 10/12 youths. The youths broke into the hotel where the asylum seekers were staying and stabbed 2 of them, of Lebanese origin."*

## FEDERAL REPUBLIC OF GERMANY

**Yet another Jewish cemetery desecrated:** Right-wing extremists are believed to be responsible for the desecration of more than 60 gravestones in a Jewish cemetery on 28.7.90 in Stuttgart. Much damage was caused and the gravestones were sprayed with Nazi symbols and grafittis like "Jews Out" and "The Gassing Never Happened".

International Herald Trib., 30.7.90*

## LAW BANNING RESIDENCE OF NON-EC NATIONALS IN CERTAIN BOROUGHS MAY BE EXTENDED

The Gol Law which authorises 6 Brussels boroughs to refuse residence registration to non-EC nationals (considered to be too numerous) is to expire in May 1990. By a large majority (44 in favour, 4 against) the borough of Schaarbeck voted to have the application of this law extended."

from La Libre Belgique 17/18 Feb. 1990*

## SWITZERLAND

**Attacks Against Asylum Seekers:** Last January, 2 asylum seekers were assailed by a group of 20 Swiss football fans in Rappergswil, Northern Switzerland. This incident followed the thrashing of the Ghanaian asylum seeker in the same town last December. The police only take action when the victim lodges a complaint, as in the case of the Ghanaian."

Neue Zurcher Zeit., 2.2.90

## FRANCE

**Paratrooper condemned to 10 years imprisonment for murder of Algerian but racist motive not accepted by Advocate General:** An ex-paratrooper has been condemned to 10 years imprisonment for the unprovoked killing of an Algerian. His accomplices received light prison terms. The plea by the lawyer of the victim's family, the Human Rights League, the Algerian League of Human Rights and an anti-racist association, MRAP, that a racist motive be retained was not accepted by the Advocate General."

Le Monde, 10.12.90*

**Protests over reception of Africans:** Strong protests were raised by the locals of a quarter of Milano against the putting up of a tent camp for 350 African immigrants in the immediate vicinity. As neither the army, nor the civil service, were in a position to arrange the camp, the project was called off by the municipality which will now look for other solutions."

La Republica, 7.2.90*

# A NATIONAL AGENDA

Whatever is said about the attitudes and aspirations of the European Parliament, the plain truth is that most of the key decisions about Europe are still being taken by national governments. This is also true of the economic, political and social conditions that black people live in within each of the Member states. There is, then, a national campaigning agenda that has to be worked upon in any effective programme to combat racism. This needs to support more localised initiatives; to affirm and apply national policies to tackle racial discrimination and inequality; and to be informed by a 'best practice' approach of our other European partners. Such an agenda can be set out under 3 broad headings -

## Personal Safety

22 **Legal protection and legal sanction against racial harassment must be strengthened.** Parliament, and individual MPs, need to be lobbied to strengthen the law, along the lines of the Dutch or Danish system: where **incitement to racial hatred and racial abuse are an offence in themselves,** not dependent upon whether you can prove that such incitement has had a clear public effect.

23 **Financial and custodial penalties associated with racial discrimination and racial attack should be increased** to ensure that positive intervention to combat racism does not get undermined by derisory sentencing powers, and that effective redress is available to the victim.

24 **Local pilot projects seeking to tackle racial harassment need to be drawn into a comprehensive national framework.** They need to be made a statutory responsibility of public authorities and **must** be able to draw on additional funding in order to deliver a **co-ordinated intervention programme** at a local level. Local authorities are the most obvious bodies to be given the lead responsibility for this by central government.

# Economic Opportunity

Much of the racism we have looked at in this Report is the direct result of appalling injustices and the super-exploitation of black people in European economies. In his book 'Lowest of the Low', Gunther Wallraff detailed part of the most obscene end of the spectrum — the treatment of Turkish guestworkers in Germany. We will never sustain a credible programme to combat racism while we condone or rely on exploitation of minorities; where neither their lives nor their livelihoods count for very much — just so long as it is beyond the public gaze. Beginning to tackle this at a national level requires important policy changes -

31 **The framework of legislation covering safety and conditions of work needs to be extended and strengthened,** particularly in respect of its application to contract and sub-contracted labour.

32 Whether by way of minimum-wage legislation or not, **a clear anti-poverty strategy needs to be developed** which has to effectively tackle the growing low pay, low skill, low prospects basis of the British economy.

33 **Britain should accept and apply the Vredling Directive concerning worker participation and information rights in employment** and include trade unions into the process of drawing up programmes to combat racism in the workplace.

34 **Government policies concerning skill training and continuing education need to be radically altered** to bring them into line with the 'best practice' of other European states. In doing so, specific support and resourcing needs to be given to **positive action training programmes** to redress discrimination and disadvantage.

35 **Parliament needs to re-examine the use of contract compliance clauses** in purchasing and tendering contracts as a means of ensuring that anti-discrimination practices are sustained equally in both public and private sectors. The government also needs to press for this to be allowed and specified in European laws governing **public procurement** policies.

36 **Specific provision needs to be fought for to enhance the rights and protection given to migrant workers:** Such protection would have to include rights to health care insurance, housing and education. It should also specify a (limited) period within which non-EC nationals in Britain become entitled to full civic and citizenship rights.

## Status

37 **The British Parliament must be made to hold itself openly accountable for the discussions and agreements it is involved in concerning citizenship rights in the UK and the European community.** It seems astonishing that Government Ministers have been allowed to proceed for so long in secret negotiations which will affect the lives and status of millions of black people in Europe. MPs must be lobbied to secure the same degree of parliamentary accountability as the Dutch have.

38 **The Government must negotiate the right of all non-EC citizens permanently resident in Britain, to have the same rights within the EC as ordinary British citizens.**

39 **Britain should develop a positive and supportive policy in relation to refugees and asylum seekers.** We could begin by taking the 'best practices' of other countries and incorporating these into comprehensive proposals which are consistent with the European Convention on Human Rights and the Refugee Charter. This must include the right of appeal and of legal representation.

40 **The same principles should be applied to a complete review of visa requirements in the UK** — removing the racist presumptions and discriminatory practices which currently apply in Britain. This should also constitute Britain's position in any negotiations about a common visa policy for the EC. The urgency of this can best be seen in the disturbing rise in the refusal rate of visa applications experienced by Commonwealth Citizens currently seeking to visit Britain.

41 Britain should require that **refugees, asylum seekers and non-EC nationals in Europe should be covered by the Social Charter.**

**42** Britain should accept, as a matter of principle, the right of family unification.

**43** Britain should oppose any moves to introduce workplace checks on immigration and nationality status.

**44** If parliament wanted to adopt the above policies it would clearly have already done so. Such changes will only come about if there is sufficient public pressure for change. **It is important that people locally and regionally -**

a) **develop their own systems of lobbying and campaigning for change,** and

b) support and contribute to the **national networks of black and anti-racist organisations** seeking to influence government policy.

## ACTION IN EUROPE

There is no point in restating the recommendations of the Ford Inquiry which we have attached as Appendix 1. These have now been presented to the European Parliament. The real battle is in terms of how many of them will be taken up and acted upon.

In essence, the battle for legal change at a European level revolves around some of the key issues we have already outlined. Both inside the European Parliament and outside it, there needs to be a sustained campaign for guaranteed legal rights for black people and migrants in Europe. These would cover

▶ rights of residence, employment, citizenship and family unification

▶ the strengthening of protection against harassment, intimidation and exploitation, and

▶ the establishment of rights of redress against discrimination in employment, training, housing, education and services.

This is the battleground of rights that has to be fought for, as much at a European as at a national and local level.

Many European MPs have been amongst the most outspoken critics of Parliamentary inactivity in the face of a rising tide of racism in Europe. But MEPs also have their own agenda — most specifically that of reducing the 'democratic deficit' which leaves the European Parliament extremely limited in terms of initiating change and introducing legislation. It is important therefore to focus on some of the key steps which MEP's and the European Parliament can also do to develop popular programmes to combat racism at a European level.

ACTION NEEDED

Saturday 1 September 1990

# Action group aims to combat attacks on Jewish targets

By Adam LeBor

JEWISH radicals are to launch a campaign against anti-Semitism and racism that will become a self-defence and vigilante force if recent attacks continue.

The move has been condemned by the Board of Deputies of British Jews, however, and further highlights the growing divisions within the 350,000-strong Jewish community over how to respond to anti-Semitism.

Since May, there have been increasing attacks on buildings and people. Cemeteries and synagogues have been vandalised in north London, Manchester and Leeds, and a holocaust memorial daubed with swastikas and the words "Jew Scum".

Jewish Action against Racism and Fascism will be launched in October. Its founders, drawn from Jewish centre-left and left-wing organisations, have been meeting throughout the summer. It is one of the initiatives being discussed by younger Jews and is indicative of a mood of growing militancy. Jewish Action's programme is likely to lead to a confrontation with community leaders.

David King, one of the organisers and a member of the Jewish Socialist Group, said: "The initial aim is to mobilise the Jewish community against anti-Semitism. JARF will be as broad-based as possible and we aim to get the board to take antisemitism more seriously and be more open about what's going on. They have a defence committee but it doesn't seem to do anything visible."

Mr King said that Jewish Action would not be a street-fighting organisation but would concentrate on organising long-term local self-defence work in areas where attacks were taking place.

"If the situation deteriorates, and there is a significant increase in the number of attacks on individual Jews and premises, we will organise self-defence patrols on a local basis by the people under threat. They are needed now in Stamford Hill. But the Jewish community cannot defend itself on its own and needs to make links with other ethnic minorities."

Jewish Action could forge a new alliance between sections of the Jewish left and the strict Orthodox community, which is also not affiliated to the Board of Deputies, but for religious rather than political reasons. Stamford Hill, in north London, home to 12,000 strictly orthodox and Hasidic Jews has recently been the scene of violence and vandalism.

The traditionally passive Hasi-

dim, recognisable because of their distinctive dress, have long been potentialtargets. But now they are drawing on the experiences of co-religionists in New York and there have been reports of physical confrontation. At least one religious leader is calling for the community to make citizens' arrests of attackers.

Rabbi Herschel Gluck said: "All we want is freedom of movement, and the ability to get on with our business without the fear of being mugged and beaten. The message to the authorities is please get something done to stop this needless fear and helplessness, because if you don't you will leave us with no alternative than to do it ourselves.

"The British legal system includes the idea of citizens' arrest and we believe in the principles of British law."

Searchlight magazine, which investigates the far right, said Nazis and a newly-established British section of the Ku Klux Klan were responsible for many of the attacks. "These are not kids, or drunks, but organised hard-line Nazis. They are redoubling their attacks, which are focusing on the Jewish community. The events in eastern Europe have given a tremendous impetus to fascist groups in western Europe."

The Board of Deputies, which has been accused of under-playing anti-Semitism, believes there is no increase in anti-Semitism, just an increase in anti-Semitic incidents, and no need for a new self-defence initiative.

Raymond Kalman, chairman of the defence committee, who earlier this week formed part of a board delegation which met David Waddington, the Home Secretary, said: "Self-defence in Stamford Hill is pure fiction, an idea in the minds of a small number of frustrated Jews who feel nobody is doing anything for them. The people talking about this are not involved in defence or security.

"They are not prepared to spend their Saturday morning standing in front of a synagogue, but when someone chucks a brick through a window they get excited." Contacts with other ethnic minorities were taking place. Mr

The Independent

82

**45** Things begin to happen in the EC when there is a **'Budget Line'** and **'Action Programme'** which the Commission has to work to. **MEPs must be pressed to make this an immediate priority in the formulation of their 1991 Budget.**

**46** **Funding for work to combat racism needs to be able to cover all aspects of personal security, access to amenities and employment, education and training, and the development of common understanding and tolerance.**

**47** **Resources and support are needed for national networks** of groups involved in work which is **seeking to combat racism, and for** those (few) organisations which have already been seeking to undertake **work on a broader European basis.**

**48** The recent **establishment of the 'European Migrants Forum',** recommended in the Evrigenis Report, **should be a priority for European funding.**

**49** The proposal to **open up the European Special Funds** to wider use, where there are particular migrant and minority population needs, should also examine ways of making support available through channels which do not depend upon the support (or sanction) of host governments. This should include provision for funding for language tuition for other than European languages.

**50** Attempts by the European Parliament to challenge the legal right of regressive proposals put forward by Member States on citizenship rights, freedom of movement, visas and treatment of refugees, should all be welcomed. But **MEPs need to be pressed to play a bigger part in organising and supporting domestic campaigns against racially discriminatory practices in their own country.**

**51** Finally, **the European Commission must provide the resources to support local action in a European context.** This may be done through 'twinning', linked campaigns, through church, community or inter-agency connections across Europe, or through the linking up of national networks of black and migrant communities. What matters is that, across Europe, a network of initiatives to combat racism is both supported **and** begins to share the lessons being learned about how best to develop such work.

The pressures of economic and environmental change are making the world a progressively smaller and more complicated place to live in. In this sense there are enormous challenges and opportunities that a 'peoples' Europe could respond to. What has to be recognised, though, is that these opportunities cannot be realised within a 'fortress Europe', mentality nor based around the creation of 'thirteenth state' within the EC — a state comprised of those who are poor, dispossessed, super-exploited, denied rights and subject to daily harassment and intimidation.

Unfortunately, such a state already exists. And large numbers of those trapped within it are black, people who provide the cheap and captive labour for dirty, dangerous jobs that no one else wants to do. It is not a question of refusing to go down this path, but of whether (and how) we can step back from it.

There is nothing sacrosanct about actions proposed in this Report. They are merely indicative of steps we must begin to take if we are to escape from a Europe caught up in a resurgent, unfettered, and market-oriented racism — a racism which, if unchecked, would cast long disfiguring shadows across the optimistic possibilities that a 'peoples Europe' holds out.

Confronting and turning back this tide, is not a challenge simply to black people in Europe, but to us all. It is a challenge we should seek to meet in the same uncompromising terms used by Lyndon Johnson in 1968 and echoed by Lord Scarman in 1981 —

> "... The only genuine , long-range solution for what has happened lies in an attack — mounted at every level — upon the conditions that breed despair and violence. All of us know what those conditions are: ignorance, discrimination, slums, poverty, disease, not enough jobs. We should attack these conditions — not because we are frightened by conflict, but because we are fired by conscience. We should attack them because there is simply no other way to achieve a decent and orderly society ...

> (quoted in Lord Scarman's Report
> into the Brixton Disorders, HMSO 1981)

A co-ordinated programme of action to tackle 'ignorance, discrimination, slums, poverty, disease, not enough jobs' would be one that black people would subscribe to — in any city in Britain, in any country in Europe. It is a programme which is long overdue.

# Appendices

# APPENDIX 1

## REPORT OF THE COMMITTEE OF INQUIRY INTO RACISM AND XENOPHOBIA
### Rapporteur: Glyn Ford MEP

### Summary of the Recommendations

#### EUROPEAN PARLIAMENT

▶ That specific responsibility for issues relating to racism, anti-semitism and xenophobia should be added to the terms of reference of the European Parliament's Committee on Legal Affairs and Citizens Rights. This would also cover all matters relating to third country nationals living in Europe.

> ▶ That at least 1 whole day per year of European Parliamentary time be set aside for a debate on racism and xenophobia within the Community.

▶ That the European Parliament set up a system for monitoring developments in respect of racism, anti-semitism and xenophobia (including the activities of extreme right and fascist groups).

> ▶ That the rights of citizens to petition the European Parliament be advertised and extended and that the Commission look into the possibility of appointing an ombudsman/woman to help resolve cases concerning racist, anti-semitic and xenophobic discrimination.

▶ That a budget line be established in the 1991 budget in order to promote and support pilot projects aimed at improving conditions and co-existence between EC nationals and legal residents from third countries.

▶ That a budget line be established in the 1991 budget and thereafter to cover positive action against racism, anti-semitism and xenophobia, with sufficient resources to deal with the seriousness of the problem. Specifically, such a budget would need to include education and the development of teaching methods that would improve people's understanding of cultural diversity.

▶ That changes in regulations should be made to allow legal residents from third countries to be eligible for employment as European Community officials.

▶ That Parliamentary groups employ within their secretariats non-Community citizens who have the right of residence within the Community.

▶ That support should be given to the European Commission's proposal for the EC's accession to the European Convention on Human Rights.

▶ That the Committee on Legal Affairs and Citizens' Rights and the Legal Service of the European Parliament seek to take legal proceedings against the European Council to ensure that the Joint Declaration Against Racism and Xenophobia, signed in June 1986, should be enforced in full.

▶ That the Committee on Legal Affairs and Citizens' Rights demand to be fully informed of the activities of the Group of Co-ordinators (The Rhodes Group) and supplied with all its working documents. In addition, the Commission and Council should be pressed to provide regular information on any discussions relating to the free movement and civil rights of residents within the European Community, or moves towards a common Community position on immigration rules, right of asylum or visa policy.

▶ That the European Parliament seek to ensure that problems relating to racism, anti-semitism and xenophobia are effectively dealt with in a co-ordinated manner. To do this they should seek the fullest co-operation with the Commission's Economic and Social Committee and with the Council of Europe.

▶ Information packs produced by the Parliament's Information Offices should include a section on racism and xenophobia, setting out Parliament's views.

## COMMISSION OF THE EUROPEAN COMMUNITIES

▶ That the President of the Commission should be asked to co-ordinate Commission activities relating to racism, anti-semitism and xenophobia and to set up an appropriate task force which covers the work of relevant Directorates-general.

▶ That a Community officer for immigration should be appointed to monitor the Commission's work and act as a contact point for immigrants.

▶ Periodic reports should be commissioned on the current situation in respect of racism, anti-semitism and xenophobia (including extreme right and fascist groups), particularly focussing on areas of high concentrations of minority communities, or those with a high level of racial tension. Such reports should be presented to the European Parliament.

▶ Proposals for legislation which are submitted by the Commission should indicate the effects that these proposals would have in combatting racism and xenophobia.

▶ Regular surveys should be conducted by Eurobarometer on the situation with regard to xenophobia and racism within the Community, and on the relations between various communities living there.

▶ An information campaign should be carried out to publicise measures designed to combat racism and xenophobia (both at Community and national level). This should set out clearly all of those bodies that members of the public may contact if they have been victims of xenophobic or racist conduct.

▶ 1995 should be designated European Year of Racial Harmony and form part of an ongoing campaign to alert residents of the community to the dangers to them all of the growth of racism, anti-semitism and xenophobia. Adequate financial resources should be made available in both 1993 and 1994 for preparation.

▶ The Commission should ensure that in all of its educational, training, youth exchange and teacher training programmes, they promote a clear European and non-discriminatory dimension. The Commission should also set up special training programmes to encourage the learning of minority languages and an appreciation of minority cultures as well as exchanges of young people from disadvantaged regions and minority communities. There should be special action programmes for Gypsies and other itinerant communities.

▶ Youth exchange programmes should be promoted in the Community to create a critical awareness among young people of past and present forms of racism, anti-semitism and fascism.

▶ The Commission should promote the development of teaching materials for schools and instructional programmes for those working with children and young people to provide instruction on racism, xenophobia and anti-semitism.

▶ The Commission should enforce the full implementation of the Council Directive on the education of children of migrant workers. This should apply to all Member States.

▶ The Commission should significantly step up efforts to enforce the full implementation of proposals concerning the education of Gypsy and traveller children.

▶ The Commission should submit a recommendation to the Council by the end of March 1991, on the role of education in combatting and preventing racism and xenophobia.

▶ Research should be promoted into the causes and forms of racism and xenophobia within the Community. Specifically this should seek to identify ways of overcoming both of these.

▶ A campaign should be conducted to raise the awareness of media professionals of the responsibilities they carry in helping with the elimination of racial and xenophobic prejudices, particularly in the way in which they deal with the news.

▶ Staff regulations applying to officials of the European Community should be opened to allow people from third countries with permanent residence status in the EC to seek employment as Community officials.

▶ The Commission should carry out and report back on a detailed study of the legislation in Member States concerning the employment of non Community citizens in their civil services.

▶ A draft directive should be prepared by the 31st March March 1991 to provide a community framework of legislation against any discrimination connected with belonging or not belonging to an ethnic group, nation, region, race or religion, covering all Community residents.

▶ A draft directive should be prepared by the 31st March 1991 to harmonize regulations throughout the Community which prohibit the dissemination of anti-semitic and racist material.

▶ A European Residents Charter be drafted, extending to residents of a Member State the right of residence and establishment in other Member States of the Community. This would also give them entitlement to a European Residents Card which would allow non Community legal residents the full freedom to circulate, to reside and to work within the European Community.

▶ A European network to combat racism and xenophobia should be promoted with community funding to allow the exchange of experience among the Member States and create points of contact for those effected.

> ▶ A Convention should be drafted on a common refugee and asylum policy building on the principles of the UN Convention on Refugees, allowing all those threatened by persecution because of their political, religious or philosophical beliefs or convictions, or gender or sexual orientation, to benefit. This should also include those who are liable to criminal prosecution for crimes that are not recognised as such within the Community. It should also apply to those liable to cruel and unusual punishment or to attack or constraint of their physical, mental or social integrity.

▶ There should be the appointment of a European Community Officer for questions of asylum.

> ▶ A directive should be drafted on the participation of recognised associations, including those of immigrants, as a third party in proceedings in which those they represent are the injured parties.

▶ The work of immigrants' advisory councils should be looked at and encouraged during a transitional phase. This should be done on an individual basis according to the quality of their record as regards democratization.

> ▶ The European Migrants Forum recommended in the Evrigenis Report should be established by the 31st December 1990.

▶ The Commission should investigate ways of bringing action in the European Court of Justice against the decisions of the Schengen states and "Ad Hoc Group on Immigration" of the Member States and then bring proceedings against them.

> ▶ In-coming Inter-governmental Conferences the Commission must assert the Community's competence in dealing with all matters relating to the harmonization of asylum rules, the removal of internal frontiers and the establishment of a Peoples' Europe. This would also cover the harmonization of entry rules and common European visa policies.

▶ The criteria relating to the European Social Fund and the European Regional Development Fund should be directed to a greater extent towards regions and localities with high immigrant populations, especially where minorities are concerned, and be applied more widely though without prejudice to the claims of the disadvantaged areas of the Community.

    ▶ There should be full support given to the Community's proposed accession to the European Convention of Human Rights.

## COUNCIL OF THE EUROPEAN COMMUNITIES

▶ The Council should reconsider its opposition to the European Community becoming a signatory of the European Convention on Human Rights.

    ▶ The Council should ensure that the European Community becomes a signatory to the UN Convention on the Elimination of all Forms of Racial Discrimination, and to the 1951 Geneva Convention on Refugees.

▶ There should be amendments to the Staff Regulations for officials of the European Communities to open the way for those from third countries with permanent resident status in one of the Community countries to permit employment as Established Community officials.

    ▶ All activities related to the free movement of third country nationals currently being dealt with in intergovernmental fora such as the Ad Hoc Group on Immigration and the Trevi working group and any other group involving all or some of the Member States of the Community should be wound up and transferred to the appropriate Community bodies.

▶ If necessary a supplementary declaration be adopted as soon as possible to the Council's Declaration against Racism and Xenophobia, expressly to give immigrants from third countries the same protection against racism and xenophobia as that afforded to citizens of the Member States.

▶ A declaration should be made that any country seeking to join the European Community must be committed to the European democratic traditions of tolerance, the elimination of all forms of discrimination connected with belonging or not belonging to an ethnic group, nation, race or religion, and be a signatory to the appropriate international and European conventions, and take steps to combat xenophobia and anti-semitism with, if necessary, denazification measures, enabling that country to meet community standards for the prevention and repression of racism and xenophobia.

▶ There should be full implementation of the Council's directive on the education of children of migrant workers. This must be seen to apply in all Member States.

## MEMBER STATES

▶ Ireland, having recently adopted legislation outlawing incitement to racial hatred, should now join other Member States as signatories to the UN Convention on the Elimination of all Forms of Racial Discrimination.

▶ An anti-discrimination law should be enacted condemning all racist acts and enabling legal persons such as associations to bring prosecutions for racist acts or to appear as joint plaintiffs.

▶ Member States should review their legislation concerning access to posts in the public services; opening up such access to nationals of third countries who have legally resided in the Member States concerned for a sufficient period.

▶ Member States should ensure that the immigrant population has access, within a reasonable period, to legal status as residents and workers.

▶ Member States should respect their commitments to ensuring that all matters relating to the removal of internal frontiers should be dealt with within the framework of the European Community's institutions. At the forthcoming Intergovernmental Conference, Member States should include an explicit statement into the treaties they sign which recognises the Community's competence in relation to third country nationals resident in the Community.

▶ Member States should work against the ghettoization of their ethnic minorities and adapt their housing policies to provide inexpensive and adequate housing to encourage integration.

▶ Member States should encourage rehabilitation programmes to improve public housing and living conditions in the cities with large immigrant population.

▶ Member States must begin to tackle the problems of immigrants' partners and family members who lose their resident status through divorce or separation. In such circumstances people should be granted independent resident status after a period of 2 years in the country, and in the case of bereavement, by granting them such status irrespective of the period of residence. In particular the right of residence of immigrant women should no longer be dependent upon that granted to the husband.

▶ Member States should review and then abolish the provisions forbidding refugees from taking up work and thus creating or fostering grounds for illegal employment.

▶ Member States should introduce legislation with severe legal sanctions, against those who employ and exploit immigrants without legal resident status. The aim of such sanctions should be the punishment of those found guilty of exploitation, not the victims of it.

▶ There should be easy and inexpensive channels through which immigrants legally resided in the Community for a continuous period of five years are able to apply for nationality status. This should apply in all Member States and not exclude dual nationality. Anyone born in a Member State should have the rights to its nationality at birth.

▶ Member States should create conditions which will enable any immigrant with legal status to learn the language of the Member States concerned.

▶ Member States should look into ways of giving the right to vote and stand (at least in local elections) first of all to Community citizens and then to all legal immigrants with five years continuous residence in that country.

▶ Member States should all set up appropriate and effective mechanisms for monitoring the strict application of conventions, resolutions and directives (and of legislation) concerning acts of racism, anti-semitism or xenophobia.

▶ Member States should respect the traditional way of life of Gypsy and other travelling communities, encouraging the provision of facilities to make this possible.

▶ Member States should encourage full and active participation by immigrant workers in trade unions.

▶ Member States should tighten up their laws aimed at repressing racism and anti-semitism.

▶ Member States should examine their own procedures for eliminating discriminatory harassment in the work of public services particularly in relation to the police and customs authorities.

▶ All Member States should undertake to fully and effectively implement the Community Directive concerning the education of children of migrant workers. This should apply equally to the children of Community and non-Community citizens resident in the EC.

▶ Member States should introduce teaching against racism in to the curriculum of their primary schools as a compulsory subject.

> ▶ Member States should adopt policies enabling children from the majority population and from ethnic minorities to be educated together.

▶ Member States should step up the support that education systems can provide for the campaign against racism, anti-semitism and xenophobia, through the teaching of human rights and history at school, through teacher training and through university research.

> ▶ Member States should ensure that information about immigrants rights, and the legal protection that they are entitled to, should be more readily available to all those who might be subject to such discrimination.

## THE MINISTERS MEETING IN POLITICAL CO-OPERATION

▶ The growth of racism, anti-semitism and xenophobia in many countries of Eastern Europe be discussed in the light of the Community's relations with them.

> ▶ The problems faced by non-Community nationals of African, Caribbean and Pacific states resident in the Community should be examined in the light of the Community's relations with these states, paying particular attention to the procedures for dialogue already established.

▶ The Foreign Ministers meeting in Political Co-operation fully discussed the implications of the recommendation that the Council make a declaration that any country seeking to join the European Community must be committed to the European democratic traditions of tolerance, the elimination of all forms of discrimination connected with belonging or not belonging to an ethnic group, nation, race or religion, and be a signatory to the appropriate international and European conventions, and take steps to combat xenophobia and anti-semitism with (if necessary) denazification measures, enabling that country to meet Community standards for the prevention and repression of racism and xenophobia.

# APPENDIX 2

## COMMON DECLARATION AGAINST RACISM

### ANIMOSITY AGAINST FOREIGNERS MUST NOT GET A CHANCE IN KARLSRUHE

*"The signs of racism and hostile behaviour are increasing in the Federal Republic of Germany. Groups and parties who are interested in racism use existing prejudices, fears and tendencies for their political targets. Real or pretended defiles and problems are traced back to a seeming imminent foreign infiltration.*

*The municipal council of Karlsruhe is watching this development with great anxiety, especially the racially and misanthropistic slogans which are told to the people by the right wing groups. The municipal council is very much against all movements to disturb the long and good corporate life between foreign fellow citizens and fellow citizens. The Municipal Council asks the population of Karlsruhe to stand up for a respectful and friendly living together of all people in this town, in our own surroundings as well as in the public.*

*Open-mindedness and respect to foreigners stood sponsor to the foundation of the city. This town would not exist without the numerous people who came from different landscapes and foreign countries to this residence. In the meantime countries and nations came together, borders and contracts lost their meaning in many things. Economic interchange, travelling and cultural relations all over the world brought foreign things to us and enriched our own life in different ways. Less than ever there is a reasonable reason nowadays to injure or to exclude people because of their origin and nationality.*

*The democratic parties of the city of Karlsruhe will prevent every start, now and in the future, to cleave asunder the German and foreign inhabitants of our town, driven by pernicious political interests. All foreigners who find reception according international law, our fundamental law, and the constitutions of the federal states in the Federal Republic of Germany, have our protection.*

*The Municipal Council's members in the city of Karlsruhe agree in their work and their aims with the demand: Animosity against foreigners must not get a chance in Karlsruhe."*

Municipal Council of the City of Karlsruhe

# Nottingham Racial Equality Council

## Stacking the Decks

A study of race, inequality and council housing in Nottingham.

**ISBN 0 9507627 0 9**   **£2.95**

## Cuckoos in the Nest?

The role of task forces in urban policy.

**£2.50**

Both titles are by Alan Simpson.

*They are available from*

Nottingham Racial Equality Council
67 Lower Parliament Street
Nottingham
NG1 3BB
Tel. 0602 586515

# Elf

SOCIALIST GROUP
EUROPEAN PARLIAMENT

## European Labour Forum

*Socialism through the back door.*

*Come in!*
*Don't bother to knock!*

**Elf** is a journal of politics edited by Ken Coates MEP.

Subscription details are available from:

Bertrand Russell House
Gamble Street
Nottingham
NG7 4ET
England

Telephone (0)602 708318
Fax (0)602 420433